Jane Goodall

Primatologist/Naturalist

Women in Science

Rachel Carson
Author/Ecologist

Dian Fossey
Primatologist

Jane Goodall
Primatologist/Naturalist

Maria Goeppert Mayer
Physicist

Barbara McClintock
Geneticist

Maria Mitchell
Astronomer

WOMEN in SCIENCE

Jane Goodall

Primatologist/Naturalist

Lisa Kozleski

CHELSEA HOUSE
PUBLISHERS
A Haights Cross Communications Company
Philadelphia

CHELSEA HOUSE PUBLISHERS
VP, NEW PRODUCT DEVELOPMENT Sally Cheney
DIRECTOR OF PRODUCTION Kim Shinners
CREATIVE MANAGER Takeshi Takahashi
MANUFACTURING MANAGER Diann Grasse

Staff for JANE GOODALL
EDITOR Patrick M. N. Stone
PRODUCTION EDITOR Jaimie Winkler
PHOTO EDITOR Sarah Bloom
SERIES & COVER DESIGNER Terry Mallon
LAYOUT 21st Century Publishing and Communications, Inc.

A Haights Cross Communications ⌐ Company

http://www.chelseahouse.com

First Printing

1 3 5 7 9 8 6 4 2

Library of Congress Cataloging-in-Publication Data

Kozleski, Lisa.
   Jane Goodall / Lisa Kozleski.
      p. cm.—(Women in science)
Summary: A biography of the zoologist, discussing her personal life
as well as her work with chimpanzees at the Gombe Stream Reserve
in Tanzania.
   ISBN 0-7910-6905-2
   1. Goodall, Jane, 1934– —Juvenile literature. 2. Primatologists—
England—Biography—Juvenile literature. [1. Goodall, Jane, 1934–
2. Zoologists. 3. Scientists. 4. Women—Biography. 5. Chimpanzees—
Habits and behavior.] I. Title. II. Series: Women in science (Chelsea
House Publishers)
QL31.G58 K69 2002
590'.92—dc21
                                                            2002015591

Table of Contents

Introduction

Jill Sideman, Ph.D.
President, Association for Women in Science

I am honored to introduce WOMEN IN SCIENCE, a continuing series of books about great women who pursued their interests in various scientific fields, often in the face of barriers erected by the societies in which they lived, and who have won the highest accolades for their achievements. I myself have been a scientist for well over 40 years and am at present the president of the Association for Women in Science, a national organization formed over 30 years ago to support women in choosing and advancing in scientific careers. I am actively engaged in environmental science as a vice-president of a very large engineering firm that has offices all around the world. I work with many different types of scientists and engineers from all sorts of countries and cultures. I have been able to observe myself the difficulties that many girls and women face in becoming active scientists, and how they overcome those difficulties. The women scientists who are the subject of this series undoubtedly experienced both the great excitement of scientific discovery and the often blatant discrimination and discouragement offered by society in general and during their elementary, high school, and college education in particular. Many of these women grew up in the United States during the twentieth century, receiving their scientific education in American schools and colleges, and practicing their science in American universities. It is interesting to think about their lives and successes in science in the context of the general societal view of women as scientists that prevailed during their lifetimes. What barriers did they face? What factors in their lives most influenced their interest in science, the development of their analytical skills, and their determination to carry on with their scientific careers? Who were their role models and encouraged them to pursue science?

Let's start by looking briefly at the history of women as scientists in the United States. Until the end of the 1800s, not just in the United States but in European cultures as well, girls and women were expected to be interested in and especially inclined toward science. Women wrote popular science books and scientific textbooks and presented science using female characters. They attended scientific meetings and published in scientific journals.

In the early part of the twentieth century, though, the relationship of women to science in the United States began to change. The scientist was seen as cerebral, impersonal, and even competitive, and the ideal woman diverged from this image; she was expected to be docile, domestic, delicate, and unobtrusive, to focus on the home and not engage in science as a profession.

From 1940 into the 1960s, driven by World War II and the Cold War, the need for people with scientific training was high and the official U.S. view called for women to pursue science and engineering. But women's role in science was envisioned not as primary researcher, but as technical assistant, laboratory worker, or schoolteacher, and the public thought of women in the sciences as unattractive, unmarried, and thus unfulfilled. This is the prevailing public image of women in science even today.

Numerous studies have shown that for most of the twentieth century, throughout the United States, girls have been actively discouraged from taking science and mathematics courses throughout their schooling. Imagine the great mathematical physicist and 1963 Nobel laureate Maria Goeppert Mayer being told by her high school teachers that "girls don't need math or physics," or Barbara McClintock, the winner of the 1983 Nobel Prize in Medicine or Physiology who wrote on the fundamental laws of gene and chromosome behavior, hearing comments that "girls are not suited to science"! Yet statements like these were common and are made even today.

I personally have experienced discouragement of this kind, as have many of my female scientist friends.

I grew up in a small rural town in southern Tennessee and was in elementary and high school between 1944 and 1956. I vividly remember the day the principal of the high school came to talk to my eighth-grade class about the experience of high school and the subjects we would be taking. He said, "Now, you girls, you don't need to take algebra or geometry, since all the math you'll need to know will be how to balance a checkbook." I was stunned! When I told my mother, my role model and principal encourager, she was outraged. We decided right then that I would take four years of mathematics in high school, and it became my favorite subject—especially algebra and geometry.

I've mentioned my mother as my role model. She was born in 1911 in the same small Southern town and has lived there her entire life. She was always an unusual personality. A classic tomboy, she roamed the woods throughout the county, conducting her own observational wildlife studies and adopting orphaned birds, squirrels, and possums. In high school she took as many science classes as she could. She attended the University of Tennessee in Knoxville for two years, the only woman studying electrical engineering. Forced by financial problems to drop out, she returned home, married, and reared five children, of whom I'm the oldest. She remained fascinated by science, especially biology. When I was in the fourth grade, she brought an entire pig's heart to our school to demonstrate how the heart is constructed to make blood circulate; one of my classmates fainted, and even the teacher turned pale.

In later years, she adapted an electronic device for sensing the moisture on plant leaves—the Electronic Leaf, invented by my father for use in wholesale commercial nurseries—to a smaller scale and sold it all over the world as part of a home nursery system. One of the proudest days of her life was when I received my Ph.D. in physical and inorganic chemistry, specializing in quantum mechanics—there's the love of mathematics again! She encouraged and pushed me all the way through my education and scientific career. I imagine that she was just like the father of Maria Mitchell, one of the outstanding woman scientists profiled in the first season of this series. Mitchell (1818–1889) learned astronomy from her father, surveying the skies with him from the roof of their Nantucket house. She discovered a comet in 1847, for which discovery she received a medal from the King of Denmark. She went on to become the first director of Vassar College Observatory in 1865 and in this position created the earliest opportunities for women to study astronomy at a level that prepared them for professional careers. She was inspired by her father's love of the stars.

I remember hearing Jane Goodall speak in person when I was in graduate school in the early 1960s. At that time she had just returned to the United States from the research compound she established in Tanzania, where she was studying the social dynamics of chimpanzee populations. Here was a young woman, only a few years older than I, who was dramatically changing the way in which people thought about primate behavior. She was still in graduate school then—she completed her Ph.D. in 1965. Her descriptions of her research findings started me on a lifetime avocation for ethology—the study of human, animal, and even insect populations and their behaviors. She remains a role model for me today.

And I must just mention Rachel Carson, a biologist whose book *Silent Spring* first brought issues of environmental pollution to the attention of the majority of Americans. Her work fueled the passage of the National Environmental Policy Act in 1969; this was the first U.S. law aimed at restoring and protecting the environment. Rachel Carson helped create the entire field of environmental studies that has been the focus of my scientific career since the early 1970s.

Women remain a minority in scientific and technological fields in the United States today, especially in the "hard science" fields of physics and engineering, of whose populations women represent only 12%. This became an increasing concern during the last decade of the 20th century as industries, government, and academia began to realize that the United States was falling behind in developing sufficient scientific and technical talent to meet the demand. In 1999–2000, I served on the National Commission on the Advancement of Women and Minorities in Science, Engineering, and Technology (CAWMSET); this commission was established through a 1998 congressional bill sponsored by Constance Morella, a congresswoman from Maryland. CAWMSET's purpose was to analyze the reasons why women and minorities continue to be underrepresented in science, engineering, and technology and to recommend ways to increase their participation in these fields. One of the CAWMSET findings was that girls and young women seem to lose interest in science at two particular points in their pre-college education: in middle school and in the last years of high school—points that may be especially relevant to readers of this series.

An important CAWMSET recommendation was the establishment of a national body to undertake and oversee the implementation of all CAWMSET recommendations, including those that are aimed at encouraging girls and young women to enter and stay in scientific disciplines. That national body has been established with money from eight federal agencies and both industry and academic institutions; it is named BEST (Building Engineering and Science Talent). BEST sponsored a Blue-Ribbon Panel of experts in education and science to focus on the science and technology experiences of young women and minorities in elementary, middle, and high school; the panel developed specific planned actions to help girls and young women become and remain interested in science and technology. This plan of action was presented to Congress in September of 2002. All of us women scientists fervently hope that BEST's plans will be implemented successfully.

I want to impress on all the readers of this series, too, that it is never too late to engage in science. One of my professional friends, an industrial hygienist who specializes in safety and health issues in the scientific and engineering workplace, recently told me about her grandmother. This remarkable woman, who had always wanted to study biology, finally received her bachelor's degree in that discipline several years ago—at the age of 94.

The scientists profiled in WOMEN IN SCIENCE are fascinating women who throughout their careers made real differences in scientific knowledge and the world we all live in. I hope that readers will find them as interesting and inspiring as I do.

1

First Contact

Most of the people whom Jane Goodall told of her plans to study the chimpanzees of Gombe in Africa thought she was crazy.

Until that time, 1960, no one had spent more than a few weeks observing chimpanzees in the wild. In the early 1920s, the psychologist Henry W. Nissen had made an attempt to study chimps in western Africa—for they are the closest animals to humans genetically—but he had learned very little during his short stay. Goodall was very different from Nissen and from most other researchers; she was an unmarried 26-year-old British woman with no college degree and very little experience in the jungle. The difference did not help her to win support for her project, and skeptics were sure the study was doomed.

But the skeptics hadn't counted on Goodall's natural curiosity and desire to learn about animals—or on Louis Leakey's confidence in Goodall and the project. Leakey, her

Jane Goodall's interest in animals began very early in life, and as a young girl in England she dreamed of going to Africa to study them. In her early twenties, she realized her goal at Gombe Stream National Park, and since that time she has become one of the world's foremost primatologists and conservationists.

mentor, whose work in Tanzania's Olduvai Gorge had transformed the theory of evolution, found an American willing to fund the study. British authorities balked at her desire to go to Africa, but they finally acquiesced when her mother—whom Nobel laureate Dr. Oscar Arias would later call "another woman of strength and wisdom"—agreed to accompany her. On May 31, 1960, with the appropriate government approvals,

Goodall and her mother, Vanne, boarded a plane to Nairobi, Kenya, and from there they continued on to Gombe Stream National Park.

What happened next has been the subject of dozens of scientific articles, popular books and films and has almost achieved the status of legend among both Goodall's supporters and her detractors. For, after several months in the jungle, after days of following the chimps silently and patiently as they went about their business and diligently recording each day's events during the night, Goodall achieved what others had thought impossible: she made contact with a wild chimp.

Goodall had seen him several times while making her observations in the jungle and had taken to calling him David Greybeard; he was a handsome chimp, by all accounts, with a distinctive bit of white hair on his chin. On November 4, just five days after her important observation of David Greybeard and a younger chimp eating meat—until that time, it was not known whether chimpanzees ate only fruits and vegetables or whether they also ate meat—Goodall saw something that made the whole excursion worthwhile: David Greybeard was using a grass stem as a tool. He had modified it into a fishing rod of sorts to withdraw termites from a mound. For an hour, he sat, fished, and happily ate the termites that clung to the grass as he pulled it from the mound. "Just two weeks before I had been told that if only I could observe a chimpanzee using a tool, then the whole study would be more than worthwhile," Goodall writes in *Reason for Hope*. "And here was David Greybeard using a tool." (66) A few days later, she saw this again, only this time she also saw how a small leafy twig was picked and then stripped of its leaves before being used as the "fishing rod." This, Goodall writes, was the crude beginning of toolmaking. "It had long been thought that we [humans] were the only creatures on earth that used and made tools. 'Man the Toolmaker' is how we were defined. This ability set us apart, it was supposed, from the rest of the animal kingdom." (67)

David Greybeard was instrumental to many of Goodall's other discoveries during that first year and in the years to come. Of all the chimps, he seemed to feel the least fear around Goodall and the other humans. Whenever he was around a group of chimps, Goodall had a better chance of approaching the rest of the group to observe them more closely before they fled in fear. As time passed, he continued to be more and more at ease around Goodall and the others in the camp. One day during that first year at Gombe, when David came into the camp to eat some bananas, he seemed especially calm. Goodall sat close beside him, and after some time passed she slowly moved her hand to his shoulder. She made a movement similar to the grooming action the chimps performed on their children and on each other. David brushed Goodall away, but very casually. So she tried again. This time, he let her groom him for about a minute before pushing her hand away again. He was a fully adult male who had lived his whole life in the wild, and he had allowed her, a human being, to touch him. To Goodall, it was "a Christmas gift to treasure." (*In The Shadow of Man*, 76)

Goodall's observations that first year at Gombe challenged human uniqueness. After she sent a telegram of the discovery of meat eating and toolmaking to Louis Leakey, he replied with the now-famous remark: "Ah! We must now redefine man, redefine tool, or accept chimpanzees as human!" (*Reason for Hope*, 67) Because of these discoveries, the National Geographic Society awarded a grant to Goodall and Leakey to continue the study, allowing her work and observations to continue.

That first grant would grow into countless more over the next 40 years, resulting in discoveries and observations that marked Goodall as one of the leading scientists and conservationists of her time. Her work with chimpanzees of Gombe distinguished her as one of the world's best-known ethologists—that is, a scientist who studies animal behavior —as well as a leading supporter of wildlife and environmental preservation. The studies she began and others continue

Goodall, who had no college education and no formal training in primatology before she went to Tanzania, seemed ill-prepared for the challenges of studying chimps in the wild. She made contact with her first wild chimp shortly after arriving in Tanzania, though, and discovered that chimps eat meat and use tools—characteristics previously thought to distinguish chimps from humans.

have changed the way people think about animals, and humankind. She has emerged as one of the world's most honored scientists and continues even today to study and write about the behavior of primates. She has founded the

Gombe Stream Research Center in Gombe Stream National Park, Tanzania, and the Jane Goodall Institute for Wildlife Research, Education, and Conservation, which is headquartered in Silver Spring, Maryland.

At the heart of all of her life's work and passion are chimpanzees. Goodall's book *The Chimpanzees I Love* is an excellent source of information about the animals she worked with for more than 40 years. The book states that chimpanzees are found in 21 African countries. They live in the west coast of the continent in countries such as Gambia, Guinea, and Liberia, and throughout countries along the equator: Gabon, Rwanda, Burundi, Congo, Uganda and Tanzania. The greatest populations of chimps live in the rain forest areas in those countries along the equator. The adult male chimps at Gombe grow to a height of about four feet and weigh as much as 115 pounds. The female chimps grow to the same height, but usually they weigh no more than 85 pounds. A female chimp in the wild usually raises two or three offspring. But female chimps have been known to raise as many as eight or nine offspring, and some have even given birth to twins.

The chimpanzees in western and central Africa are a bit bigger and heavier than those at Gombe. Chimps kept in captivity—such as in zoos or in scientific laboratories—are often heavier too. Chimps in the wild can live as many as 50 years, while those in captivity have lived more than 60 years.

The scientific name for chimpanzee is *Pan troglodytes* ("pan trog-low-*die*-tees"). Chimps are primates, like gorillas and humans, and are similar physically to lemurs, monkeys, apes, and humans. Apes are very much like humans and have no tails. They are divided into the *lesser* apes—gibbons and siamangs—and the *great* apes—orangutans, chimpanzees, bonobos and gorillas. Humans are a kind of great ape. Scientists believe that primates descended from small, insect-eating mammals that walked the earth more than 65 million years ago and that apes and humans descend from a common ancestor that lived about 15 to 20 million years ago.

The ape that is most like a human is the chimpanzee; in fact, a chimpanzee is far more like a human than it is like a gorilla. The DNA, or genetic code, of chimps differs from human DNA by just over one percent—so genetically chimps and humans are 99% the same. That's why chimps are used in medical research. Humans can receive blood donated by chimps, and chimps can catch, or be given, all the infectious diseases that humans catch.

Throughout her decades at Gombe, Goodall learned more about chimpanzees than had ever been known before. And during that time, although she has come to know dozens of chimps over time in Africa, it is David Greybeard who still holds one of the most important positions in Goodall's heart. His death touched Goodall in a way the deaths of any other chimp did not—and she spoke gratefully of him, and his gentle, trusting nature, long after he was gone. "Of all the Gombe chimpanzees, though, it is David Greybeard whom I have loved the most," Goodall writes in *Through a Window*. (240) "His body was never found. He simply stopped coming to camp and, as the weeks became months, we gradually realized that we would never see him again. Then I felt a sorrow deeper than that which I have felt for any other chimpanzee, before or since. I am so glad I was spared the anguish I should have known had I seen him, too, in death. David Greybeard, gentle yet determined, calm and unafraid, David Greybeard who opened my first window into a chimpanzee's world."

That world was a long way from Goodall's home in England. But by opening a window into a chimpanzee's world for Goodall, people around the globe now have had the chance to glimpse the rare, the wild, and the unknown, all of which exist in a national park in the heart of Africa, and in the heart of a woman named Jane Goodall.

Although she began with a love of animals and moved from there into primatology, Dr. Goodall's mission has expanded to encompass the preservation of all of nature. She now works with organizations in Africa and around the world to promote more eco-friendly ways of organizing human life, and one of her current goals is to draw the world's youth into the effort. She is shown here receiving an "eco-hero" award in 1998.

2

Life Before Africa: 1934–1957

THE BIRTH OF A SCIENTIST

Named Valerie Jane Morris-Goodall at her birth on April 3, 1934, in London, England, she was the older of two daughters born to Margaret Myfanwe ("Vanne") Joseph and Mortimer ("Mort") Herbert Morris-Goodall. Her father was working as a telephone cable-testing engineer in London when Jane was born, but his true passion was fast, well-engineered racecars. He later became a racecar driver and competed with Britain's Aston Martin team against French, Italian and German teams. Goodall writes in *My Life with the Chimpanzees* that she remembered very little of her father's fast-paced, mechanical life, and instead received the love, influence and respect for the natural world from her mother and her beloved nanny, Nanny Sowden.

Vanne and Nanny introduced Jane to a world of gardens, flowers, birds, sunlight, warm winds, and pets—and of respect for nature, animals, and other people. In *Africa in My Blood*, an

Goodall's early experience in Germany was less than ideal, but it was important, for her reaction to seeing the spires of the great cathedral at Cologne soaring over the ruins of that war-torn city codifies the idea behind her later work: "To me," she said, "it seemed like a message from God, telling us that however bad things may seem, in the end, goodness will always win."

edition of Goodall's letters, editor Dale Peterson writes that Goodall received the best of both her parents. From her father, she inherited a strong constitution, including focus of intent, endurance, an iron stomach, a minimal appetite, and excellent eyesight. From her mother, Goodall received a certain sensibility, including sociability, effective habits of observation, and a love of literature. "But who would have imagined how successfully she would gather those gifts in pursuit of her life's goal?" Peterson writes. (4)

And Goodall has loved and been intrigued by animals for as long as she can remember. In *My Life with the Chimpanzees*, she recounts an incident that took place in 1939, when she was 5 years old and England was at war with Germany—a tale that foretells the patience and curiosity that would make all her later work possible. Seized with a desire to determine the origin of eggs, she crept into the henhouse, concealed herself as best she could, and watched the hens intently. "It was very stuffy and hot where I crouched and the straw tickled my legs," she writes. "There was hardly any light, either. But I could see the bird on her nest of straw. She was about five feet away from me, on the far side of the chicken house, and she had no idea I was there. If I moved I would spoil everything. So I stayed quite still. So did the chicken." (*My Life with the Chimpanzees*, 1)

The young Goodall saw the chicken raise herself up from the straw and, as the chicken faced Goodall, a round white object began to emerge from between the chicken's legs. The new-laid egg soon landed in the straw—and Goodall had seen the whole thing. Thrilled, she raced back to the house, where she found her mother on the verge of calling the police; Goodall had been missing for hours, her mother totally unaware that she had camped out in the henhouse to find out where eggs came from. In her autobiography, Goodall writes: "How lucky it was that I had an understanding mother! Instead of being angry because I had given her a scare, she wanted to know all about the wonderful thing I had just seen." (*My Life*, 2) Goodall told her mother how she had wondered where on a chicken was an opening big enough for an egg to come out, and she decided to find out for herself. After scaring a few hens away when she tried to follow them into the henhouse, she realized she would have to sneak into the henhouse before any of the chickens were in there, and wait for nature to take its course. The lesson she learned: "You have to be patient if you want to learn about animals." (*My Life*, 2) Throughout her childhood, Goodall had many opportunities to witness animal behavior, and these experiences would shape her and direct her toward her later work.

THE BIRCHES AND THE ANIMALS

After leaving London as a young child, Goodall and her family—which by then included her younger sister, Judy—moved briefly to France. Goodall's parents wanted the girls to grow up speaking French, but a few months after they arrived, Hitler began a series of invasions that would lead to World War II, so the family returned to England. Since they had sold their house, they went to live in the old manor house in which Goodall's father had been raised. The property around the manor house included ruins from a castle where King Henry VIII had locked away one of his six wives. In addition to the history of the property, there were also many animals in and around the manor house—more than six geese near the house, five henhouses, and cows in a nearby field. Racehorses also grazed in the meadows near the house; they were the passion and business of Goodall's father's brother, her uncle Rex. Rex taught Goodall to ride when she was just two years old, on a horse named Painstaker.

Goodall did not stay too long at the manor house, however, as her father had enlisted in the Army to fight in the war, and Goodall's nanny was married and left the family. Goodall, Judy, and their mother went to live with Goodall's maternal grandmother, whom they called Danny, in a house called The Birches in Bournemouth, on the southern coast of England, just a few minutes' walk from the English Channel. The family shared the house with Goodall's two aunts, Olly and Audrey, and an uncle who came home most weekends. In addition, because of the war, families who had homes were asked to take in people who did not have a place to live, and so for many years, two single women lived at The Birches as well.

Goodall learned about animals through direct experience. She took riding lessons, eventually getting proficient enough to take others out for rides and compete in horse shows. Her relationship with animals was strong even in her childhood.

Goodall attended the English version of primary school and junior high and high school in Bournemouth. In her autobiography, she writes that she never really liked school. But she still did very well, especially in subjects she found most interesting—English, history, Scripture, and biology. She said she didn't mind the work, but she hated being indoors instead of outside, where she savored horseback writing, spending time in the garden, or walking along the beach. In the winter, she liked to read. She was a regular visitor to the library, and devoured books such as Hugh Lofting's *The Story of Doctor Dolittle*, which included tales of Africa. Goodall decided then and there that she would one day go to Africa. She was seven years old.

Goodall also liked books about animals—tales of wolves, bears, and wolverines in North America, snakes and sloths in

South America, and orangutans and elephants in Asia. She loved Rudyard Kipling's *The Jungle Book*, Kenneth Grahame's *The Wind in the Willows*, and all Edgar Rice Burroughs' Tarzan books. As much as Goodall loved reading about animals, though, she knew she couldn't yet see them, for there were no zoos nearby and leaving home was not yet an option. But she also knew she wanted to see animals in their natural habitat. So she started studying the animals that frolicked in her own neighborhood—squirrels, birds, snails, and bugs. She also started a nature club with her sister and their closest friends, Sally and Sue Cary. As she grew older, Goodall spent more time working with horses and riding. Every Saturday during the school year and twice a week during vacations, she would take riding lessons at the stable of Miss Bush. Eventually, she became skilled enough to work in the stables, take clients out for rides, and even compete in horse shows.

Throughout her childhood, Goodall's most trusted companion was a black spaniel-mix dog named Rusty. He lived with his owner in a hotel near The Birches but was a faithful friend to Goodall. He proved himself to be a quick learner as Goodall instructed him in "shaking," sitting with a biscuit on his nose, playing dead, and jumping through hoops. She rewarded him with praise—almost never with food. Rusty lived at the hotel, but came to The Birches at 6:30 each morning. He returned to the hotel to eat his dinner, but would quickly trot back to Goodall's home for the rest of the evening. "Rusty taught me so much about animal behavior, lessons I have remembered all my life," writes Goodall in her auto-biography. (*My Life*, 22) "He taught me that dogs can think things out—that they can reason. . . . Rusty was the only dog I have ever known who seemed to have a sense of justice. If he did something he *knew* was wrong (that is, something I had taught him was wrong), then he apologized the way dogs do, by rolling on his back and grinning. But if I was cross about something *he* thought was okay, then he sulked."

"SIGNS OF WAR WERE ALL AROUND"

As Goodall grew up, the war was raging. It left a lasting mark on the young girl. She remembers hearing the droning of German planes and the sound of exploding bombs near The Birches in Bournemouth. (*Reason for Hope*, 12) She also remembers the sound of the air-raid warnings: "They usually sounded some-time in the night, for that was when the bombers came over. (*Reason*, 12) Then we had to leave our beds and huddle together in a little air-raid shelter that was erected in our house in the small room (once a maid's bedroom) that, even today, is known as the 'air-raid.'" Goodall said that by the time she was seven, she was accustomed to news about battles—both defeats and victories—as well as stories of man's inhumanity to man. This, too, would stay with her throughout her life:

> Although my own life was filled with love and security, I was slowly becoming aware of another kind of world altogether, a harsh and bitter world of pain and death and human cruelty. And although we were among the luckiest, far away from the horror of massive bombings, never-theless, signs of war were all around: Our own father, far away and in uniform, somewhere in the jungles of Singapore. . . . The blackout that dominated our lives every evening. The American soldiers with their tanks who occupied the road outside The Birches. One of them became a real friend, but then went off to the front with his regiment and was, like many so many hundreds, killed.
>
> (*Reason*, 12–13)

The war years and those that followed took a personal toll on the family as well: Goodall's uncle Rex, a member of the Royal Air Force, was killed in a collision in 1942, and Goodall's parents, separated throughout the 1940s, saw their marriage fall apart when Mort returned to civilian life in 1951. Still, letters that were kept by friends and family of show that Goodall's childhood was essentially happy, that she was an exuberant, enthusiastic, intelligent girl growing into a woman. By the time she finished high school in 1952, she knew what she wanted to do—watch and write about animals. But she wasn't yet sure how she would accomplish that goal, much less how to earn a living doing it.

Although Goodall had done well enough in school to attend a university, the family could not afford the tuition. To be eligible for a scholarship, students needed to know a foreign language, and in her own opinion Goodall was never very good at these. At this crossroads, Goodall's mother urged her to learn some practical skills. So from September to December of 1952, Goodall went to Germany with the idea of learning German while living with a family. According to her autobiography, Goodall's mother felt it was important for Goodall to know that although Hitler and the Nazis were evil and brought much pain to so many people, ordinary Germans existed who were not like Hitler. Goodall found the she didn't enjoy the visit much, and wasn't very successful at learning German—it didn't help that the members of her host family were so eager to practice English that they spoke very little German. So she returned to The Birches in time for Christmas. But one part of her visit left an important mark on Goodall. It happened when she visited the city of Cologne. In her autobiography, Goodall writes that like many other German cities, Cologne had been heavily bombed during the war. But the graceful spires of Cologne Cathedral rose undamaged from the flattened battered city surrounding it. "To me it seemed like a message from God, telling us that however bad things may seem, in the end, goodness will always win," she writes. (*My Life*, 26)

After returning from Germany, Goodall decided to attend secretarial school in London; her mother had told her that secretaries could find employment anywhere in the world. In May of 1953, she rented a room from the mother of her mother's friend and began her studies in typing, shorthand, and bookkeeping at Queen's Secretarial College in South Kensington. Goodall writes that she loved being in London, where she regularly visited the museums and attended concerts. She also dated several young men during this time, and they would take her out to dinner or to see plays. "I had never had time for boys before," Goodall writes. "I had been far too busy with horses and walking in the country and Rusty. But now I had left school and was out in the big world." (*My Life*, 26–27)

"OUT IN THE BIG WORLD"

A year later, Goodall had finished her studies and returned to The Birches to clean out her old bedroom in preparation of finding a job in Oxford, home to one of England's two famous universities. But first, she spent a six months doing clerical work at her aunt Olly's clinic, where she worked as a physiotherapist to children in the Bournemouth region. Goodall's job was to type letters, but she saw and got to know many of the disabled children who were being treated at the clinic. Their problems ranged from babies born with clubfeet to children who had been paralyzed from polio to young adults who were facing death because of muscular dystrophy. Goodall writes that she learned a great deal at the clinic. In particular, she said that ever since then, whenever she has had problems in her life, she remembered how lucky she was to be healthy. In addition, she said she has since then felt a special closeness with people who are disabled.

After leaving Olly's clinic, Goodall did find a job working for the Oxford University Registry in Oxford by August of 1954. Her office was located in a beautiful old building dating to the 18th century, and her immediate supervisor let Goodall bring her pet hamster, Hamlette, to work. Goodall says the job itself was terribly boring, but she had great fun getting to know the other students and spending time along the river. While in Oxford, she learned to punt—that is, propel a long, flat-bottomed boat along the river while pushing with a pole—and, dressed and feeling like a princess, she attended several of the famous "May Balls."

After spending a year at Oxford, Goodall returned to London, where she found work at a film studio that produced

In her childhood, Goodall and other members of her family lived with Goodall's maternal grandmother in a house called The Birches in Bournemouth, England, near the English Channel. One of her favorite companions there was Rusty, a dog who lived nearby; she learned much from him about animal behavior.

documentaries. Her specific job involved choosing the music for films, and she learned how to edit, make sound tracks, mix and other aspects of filmmaking. At this time, she lived in her father's apartment in London; for, apparently, Goodall's parents remained good friends after their divorce. While she enjoyed getting to know her father a bit better during that time, there was still something missing: her dreams of Africa. She still spent her free time walking through the Natural History Museum, and continued to read books about animals, especially those in Africa.

And then, all of a sudden, Goodall had a chance to see her dreams become a reality. On December 18, 1956, she received a letter from her best friend from school, Marie-Claude Mange—better known as Clo. Goodall hadn't heard from her for quite some time, and so she was surprised to see that the letter was postmarked from Africa. As Goodall recounts in *Reason for*

Hope, Clo writes that her parents had just bought a farm in Kenya, and she wanted to know if Goodall would be interested in coming to the continent for a visit. Goodall was overcome with excitement and disbelief, and instantly began working to

DR. GOODALL DESCRIBES THE CHIMPANZEE

From "Life and Death at Gombe":

Their life expectancy is probably between 40 and 50 years in the wild. The females give birth only once in five or six years (unless a baby dies, and then the mother usually conceives again within a few months). Also, there is such individual variation among them that a very long-term study is necessary if we are to understand their behavior. . . .

The structure of the chimpanzee brain is amazingly close to our own. The chimpanzee life cycle is not very different from ours—five years of infancy, then a period of childhood, followed by adolescence from about 9 to 14 years. Old age sets in at about 35 years. As among humans, affectionate and supportive bonds between mothers and their children, and between siblings, may persist throughout life.

Chimpanzees use more objects as tools and for more purposes than any creatures except ourselves. They may show cooperation when hunting for food, and when a kill is made . . . adults may share the prize. . . . Friendly social gestures include holding hands, patting one another, embracing, and kissing. Those who have worked closely with chimpanzees agree that their emotions . . . seem very similar to our own, though this is difficult to prove.

"Life and Death at Gombe,"
National Geographic, 1979.

A letter from a school friend, inviting her to the Mange family's farm, offered to Goodall the chance to turn her dreams of Africa into a reality. After months of saving money—followed by nearly a month of travel—Goodall arrived in Kenya on her 23rd birthday.

save the money needed for the round-trip ticket. Goodall had to quit her job at the filmmaking studio, because it did not pay enough for her to save any funds—and she turned in her letter of resignation on the day she received Clo's letter. She returned to her family's home in Bournemouth so she could live at home while she saved her money. She worked as a waitress, saving every penny she could. It took her five months of grueling hours and hard work before she had enough saved up. At last, Goodall writes in *Reason for Hope*, "I could go to Africa—and my life would be changed forever." (35)

3

The Beginning of the Work: 1957–1961

THE ARRIVAL IN KENYA

Goodall departed for Africa on a passenger liner called the *Kenya Castle,* which traveled for 21 days down the western coast of Africa, stopping now and then in the Canary Islands. Next, the boat cruised past the Cape of Good Hope and stopped at Cape Town and Durban before docking for good on April 2, 1957 at Mombasa, the coastal port of Kenya. Goodall loved the sea air, and unlike many passengers who spent much of the trip down below in their cabins, Goodall thrived on the deck— especially in rough weather. She spent countless hours watching the dolphins, sharks, and fish and keeping track of the moving sea.

From Mombasa, Goodall took a two-day train ride to Kenya's capital city, Nairobi. She arrived on her 23rd birthday, April 3, 1957. There, she was met by Clo Mange, Clo's father, Roland, and another friend. As the group traveled to the Mange

Goodall has established a rapport with her chimpanzees over the years. The most important thing in her early research was not to be seen as an intruder—not to disturb the chimps' natural patterns of life. It took some time for her to find that equilibrium.

farm, where Goodall was to stay for three weeks, Goodall caught her first glimpse of a giraffe up close. In her autobiography, *My Life with the Chimpanzees*, Goodall remembers the giraffe's long legs and beautiful dark, thick-lashed eyes. The giraffe had been chewing on acacia thorns but, on seeing that he was observed, turned and ran away in slow motion. "When I saw him, that amazing long, long animal, I finally knew, for sure, that I was really there," Goodall writes in *My Life*. "I had actually gotten to the Africa of my dreams—the Africa of Doctor Dolittle and Tarzan." (34)

Goodall and Clo enjoyed three weeks together at Greystones, her family's farm. Greystones was near the tiny trading center Naivasha, which itself was located in a part of Kenya called the Kinankop, or the White Highlands. After leaving the farm,

On the way to the Mange farm, Goodall sighted a giraffe—the first giraffe that she had ever seen, and among the first exotic animals—and felt that she was really living her dream at last.

Goodall moved to Nairobi to begin working in a temporary job; not wanting to take advantage of her friend's generosity, she'd found work in Africa even before her departure from England. She worked in a large company, and although the job was not exciting, it allowed her to earn money and look for a way to work with animals.

LOUIS LEAKEY

It took less than two months of talking with various people about her dreams for her to find that way. Clo and her father at last directed her, if she was interested in animals, to meet a man named Louis Leakey. Leakey was a famous anthropologist—a specialist in the study of people—and paleontologist—a specialist in the early development of humans. Goodall made an appointment to meet him and went to his office on May 24. "The meeting was momentous, arguably the most important event of Goodall's Kenya Colony experience," writes Dale Peterson in *Africa in My Blood*. (83) That meeting was the first step in the journey of Goodall's life's work. And at the center of it all was the extraordinary Louis Leakey.

By the time Goodall met him, Leakey had already established himself and his reputation in the field of anthropology. He and his second wife, Mary, had started digging up ancient stone tools and fossilized bones and skull fragments at Olduvai Gorge. His studies also focused on the life patterns of the great apes—chimpanzees, gorillas and bonobos in African forests—and their similarities to the behaviors of early humans. He was looking for protégés to embark on thorough study of the various species of ape.

According to Peterson's book, Goodall was ideally suited for Leakey's project, for she shared with Leakey "a powerful fascination with animals and nature, an interest in paleoanthropology, an exceptional energy, endurance and fortitude. Her lack of any formal training was an advantage, in his view, for it meant that she could begin her studies without any foolish academic preconceptions. That she was a woman was also positive, Leakey believed, for a woman would be less threatening to a male-dominated ape community." (*Blood*, 84) "Louis Leakey . . . didn't get on so well with men," recalled Goodall in a 1999 interview. "He felt he related more easily to women and that women made better observers." Letters from Goodall also mention that Leakey was initially romantically attracted to Goodall—as he had been, it seems, to other bright young women. She rebuffed his advances repeatedly, though, and eventually they were able to establish the even working relationship that would last until Leakey's death in 1972.

This relationship began with Leakey's offering Goodall a job at their first meeting—his secretary had just resigned. But before they started working in the museum, Leakey and his wife, the anthropologist Mary Leakey, took Goodall and another young woman who worked at the museum on a trip to Olduvai Gorge in Tanganyika. At that time, few white people had seen the Gorge. There wasn't even a road leading there—just the trail of faint tire marks that the Leakeys themselves had left the year before. It was a long trip, but they finally arrived; they spent three months there, looking for fossils during the day and sleeping in tents at night. Again, Goodall found the experience overwhelmingly exciting: that first night, as they sat around the campfire eating meals out of tins, she heard the distant roar of a lion, and later that night she heard a hyena. "I had never been so happy," she writes. (*My Life*, 37) "There I was, far, far from any human dwellings, out in the wilds of Africa, with animals all around me in the night. Wild, free animals. That was what I had dreamed of all my life."

LIFE AT OLDUVAI GORGE

The work was not easy. The hot sunlight beat on their backs as they worked on the Serengeti Plain. Searching for fossils involved a lot of digging and chipping with picks and shovels through layers of soil. But as she chipped away at the earth, Goodall felt a sense of awe, and the work led her to a greater understanding of history. When the three-month project was complete, she found it hard to leave, but she consoled herself with the knowledge that she would soon be working at the museum with the Leakeys.

Louis Leakey was a leading anthropologist and paleontologist when he met Jane Goodall; he was already famous for his work with early human remains in Tanzania's Olduvai Gorge. Goodall, like several other notable scientists, benefited from Leakey's influence, for he had sufficient prestige to secure funding for extensive research projects. She moved away from his work in the end, though, preferring live animals to dead ones.

When she returned to Nairobi, Goodall moved into one of the staff apartments at the museum. Her childhood friend Sally came from England to share the apartment with her for an extended visit. Soon the two friends started collecting animals that had been orphaned, abandoned, or rescued from African markets, and before long their apartment was a menagerie. Their first furry pet was named Levi. He was a small galago—a bush baby, a small, squirrel-like animal related to a monkey. During the day, Levi slept in a large gourd on top of a cupboard in Leakey's office, and at night he would run around the room catching bugs that had been attracted to the lights. Their next pet was a vervet monkey named Kobi, and this was followed by a dwarf mongoose they called Kip. After these two came a partner for Kobi, Lettuce, and a partner for Kip, Mrs. Kip. The roommates also kept a hedgehog and a black and white rat rescued from the school at which Sally sometimes taught. In addition to these more unusual pets, they had a cocker spaniel and a springer spaniel, Tana and Hobo, and a Siamese cat named Nanky-Poo.

THE LEAKEYS: "The First Family of Paleontology"

When Fossey met Louis Leakey, he had already achieved a cult following in the United States; his family has gone on to become synonymous with paleontology, the study of prehistoric life.

Louis S.B. Leakey (1903–1972) was a native of Kenya, born to British missionaries. He grew up in an area in which stone tools could be found accidentally and studied anthropology at Cambridge. In 1926, he accompanied an expedition to Tanzania—later the land of Jane Goodall's research—as an expert on Africa; he worked in Tanzania to prove Charles Darwin's theory that man's origin was to be found there, and not in Asia as many believed. His first visit to Olduvai Gorge, the site of his most famous discoveries, was in 1931.

He met Mary Douglas Nichols, herself of a rare anthropological background, on a dig in England, and the two worked on the same projects in Tanzania for some time before their marriage. Their son Richard, born in 1944, found his own first fossil at the age of six, was leading digs by 1963, and was head of the National Museum of Kenya a few years after that.

Immersed in her work, her pets, and her friends, Goodall was enjoying life thoroughly. By September of 1958, she had saved enough money to fly her mother to Africa for a visit. Her mother loved Africa immediately, as Goodall had thought she would, and she quickly warmed to Goodall's friends and made friends of her own. While visiting Nairobi, she and her daughter talked a great deal about Jane's future. Leakey never cared whether members of his staff had a college education, Goodall writes; all that mattered to him was that they be knowledgeable, hardworking, and dedicated. She could stay at the museum as

In 1959, searching for the first tool-using humans, the shy and scientifically rigorous Mary found a skull from a genus she called "Zinj" (*Zinjanthropus*). The exhibition of the skull brought to the Leakeys fame and, more important, financial support— and the couple parted to work independently. Mary continued at Olduvai Gorge, and Louis lectured to raise money, also launching the work of Jane Goodall with chimpanzees, Dian Fossey with gorillas, and Birute Galdikas with orangutans.

After Louis Leakey's death in 1972, Mary, Richard, and Meave Leakey (Richard's wife, also a paleontologist) continued to make important discoveries and to work toward mapping the complexities of human evolution. In 1978, Mary Leakey discovered the fossilized footprints of a pre-human species, thereby completely altering the model of the evolution of upright walking and suggesting a new species to be added to the evolutionary "family tree." She died in 1996, and now Richard and Meave's daughter Louise has joined the effort. The Leakeys' work has changed, even defined, paleontology, and they will forever be considered its "first family."

long as she wanted. She also could study fossils and start working full-time on projects such as the work she'd done with the Leakeys at Olduvai Gorge. Still, neither path seemed quite right for her:

> . . . [B]oth of those careers had to do with dead animals. And I still wanted to work with living animals. My childhood dream was as strong as ever: Somehow I must find a way to watch free, wild animals living their own, undisturbed lives. I wanted to learn things that no one else knew. Uncover secrets through patient observation. I wanted to come as close to talking to animals as I could. . . . I wanted to move among them without fear, like Tarzan.
>
> (*My Life*, 46)

So Goodall decided to act on her dreams again. Although she had no training or experience, she approached Leakey to tell him she would be very much interested in a project he had discussed with her casually from time to time—a long-term study of some chimpanzees living on the shores of Lake Tanganyika in western Tanzania. His response was just what she wanted to hear: "I've been waiting for you to tell me that. Why did you think I talked about those chimpanzees to you?" (*My Life*, 48) He warned her that it would not be an easy project and that he would first need to find money even to bring it into being. He suggested that she return to England in the meantime to learn as much as she could about chimps, so Goodall and her mother returned by ship, through the Suez Canal, with stops at Aden and Barcelona. By the time she returned to England, around Christmas of 1958, she had traveled around the whole continent of Africa and was ready for the next step: learning about chimpanzees.

LEARNING ABOUT CHIMPANZEES

More than a year would pass before Goodall began her work with the chimps of Gombe. In England she took a position at the library of the London Zoo, and there she spent countless hours watching the three chimpanzees the zoo kept. It was heartbreaking for Goodall to see them caged—she writes that one chimp seemed to have gone mad from being shut up in a small cage so long—and she promised herself that she would one day improve conditions for chimps in captivity. She read as much as she could about chimps—but everything that had been written was about chimps in labs, or chimps that had been kept in people's homes. Little work had been done, if any at all, on chimps as they lived in the wild.

While in London, Goodall met a charming, handsome actor named Robert Young. The two quickly fell in love and decided to get married. Their engagement announcement appeared in the social section of two newspapers on May 13, 1960—just as Leakey was writing to say that he had received permission from the Tanganyika Game Department for Goodall to study Gombe's chimps and that he'd found grant money to support her research. The wedding plans were put on hold, and over the next few months they were called off.

On May 31 of that year, Goodall and her mother got on a plane to Nairobi; the government required that Goodall travel with a female companion, and her mother had been happy to oblige. In Africa, Dr. Leakey greeted them with bad news: a dispute among the fishermen camping along the shore of Lake Tanganyika had made conditions unsafe for the two women. While they waited for local politics to simmer down, Goodall and her mother traveled to Lake Victoria, where Goodall could watch vervet monkeys. This short study of monkeys, Goodall writes, prepared her for her work with the chimps, as it taught her everything from how to take notes in the field and what clothing to wear to what kinds of movement a monkey will tolerate from a human.

By June 30, mother and daughter had received permission to travel to Gombe. They made the 800-mile trip by car, arriving in the town of Kigoma on July 8, 1960. They took a

The United Republic of Tanzania. The area of Ngorongoro Crater, a vast wildlife preserve, is not far from the Kenyan border or the Serengeti Plain. Mount Kilimanjaro, the highest mountain in Africa, is to the east. Gombe is located in the far west of the country, on Lake Tanganyika, between the city of Kigoma and the Burundian border. Kigoma is the closest city to Gombe.

small boat to Gombe on July 14 with a cook and the game ranger of the chimpanzee reserve—about 20 square miles that was home to about 160 different chimps, and other primates, too, including olive baboons; red colobus monkeys; blue, red-tailed, and vervet monkeys; and others. Goodall sighted her first chimp on her first day at Gombe, but it would be many months before her first true discoveries—the toolmaking and "fishing" of David Greybeard and the omnivorousness of chimps in general.

Goodall and her mother both battled malarial fever for a while, but they recovered in short order, and Goodall's research began to take shape. In early October of 1960, Goodall and her mother were visited by the distinguished field zoologist George B. Schaller and his wife, Kay. The couple had just finished a pioneering study of mountain gorillas in Rwanda. In a letter Goodall wrote in October, she credits Schaller with a challenge that would shape her research: "George said he thought that if I could see chimps eating meat, or using a tool, a whole year's work would be justified." (*Blood*, 155) Before three weeks had passed, Goodall observed both.

Perhaps the most significant achievement of the year, though, was Goodall's success in overcoming the animals' natural fear of her presence. Peterson describes her achievement:

> By moving among the wild chimpanzees and immersing herself as fully as possible into their world, this young, scientifically naïve woman had chosen to sail right off the edge of the map, to enter the *terra incognita* of scientific research. The results were astonishing. By her 27th birthday . . . a few of the apes were actually wandering into camp.
>
> (*Blood*, 156)

This success was not simply a matter of luck; Goodall had worked very hard to achieve this state, following the chimps slowly and silently as they moved through the forest, wearing

Goodall worked hard to establish a sense of trust with the chimps she observed, and she was able to make contact with many of them. Her adaptation to their behavioral patterns was so complete that she felt she could actually understand their motivations and "think like a chimp."

dull-colored clothes, and acting only in non-threatening ways. By July of 1961, at the end of her first year at Gombe, she had met the challenge: the hills and the forest had become her home. More important, in Goodall's own opinion, was that her mind had begun to work more like a chimp's mind, at least unconsciously.

4

Establishment: 1961–1967

It is not easy to study emotions even when the subjects are human. As we try to come to grips with the emotions of beings progressively more different from ourselves the task, obviously, becomes increasingly difficult. If we ascribe human emotions to nonhuman animals we are accused of being anthropomorphic—a cardinal sin in ethology. But is it so terrible? If we test the effect of drugs on chimpanzees because they are biologically so similar to ourselves, if we accept that there are dramatic similarities in chimpanzee and human brain and nervous system, is it not logical to assume that there will be similarities also in at least the more basic feelings, emotions, moods of the two species?
—Jane Goodall, *Through a Window*, (1987)

CREATING A SCIENTIFIC REPUTATION

Goodall moved to a studio apartment on Magrath Avenue in Cambridge in December of 1961 and took part in traditional university activities—lectures, meeting with her advisors,

Gombe Stream National Park became "home base" for Goodall's observation efforts and the site of many of her discoveries. Research continues there to this day, and visitors are welcome to make observations of their own.

writing papers—as well as some unusual ones. She was invited to scientific conferences in London and New York to discuss her findings at Gombe, and she submitted papers for publication in scientific journals. She finished her first term at Cambridge in June of 1962, and was back at Gombe in July.

She stayed in Africa again until December of 1962, this

time working on communicating her discoveries with the outside world through writing and photography. The National Geographic Society, based in Washington, D.C., had begun to support her work at Gombe in 1961. That year, editors approached Leakey about the possibility of an article about Goodall, with plenty of the photographs for which the society's magazine, *National Geographic*, is famous. It was difficult to find someone suitable for the difficult job of photographing the chimps, and it wasn't until Goodall returned to Africa, in the summer of 1962, that a willing and able wildlife photographer was found. This talented photographer, a Dutch baron named Hugo van Lawick, would join forces with Goodall for far more than just a magazine article.

BARONESS VAN LAWICK-GOODALL

By the end of the summer, van Lawick had taken enough superb photographs for *National Geographic* to proceed with the article on Goodall and her work. Goodall finished her first draft of the article in December of 1962. By August of 1963, "My Life Among the Wild Chimpanzees" had been published in three million copies of the glossy magazine. Goodall's article was accompanied by three dozen of van Lawick's photographs, including one of a chimpanzee carrying meat and another of three chimps using twigs to "fish" for termites.

In the article, Goodall writes "I must say . . . that through-out the . . . study of the chimps at the Gombe Stream, I have often felt like an anthropologist taking notes on a tribe of people, for chimpanzees can seem so human." (*Blood*, 232) Indeed, she gave human names to many of the chimps, such as Flo, David Greybeard, and David's friend Goliath. This attitude was not warmly accepted in the scientific community at that time—the concern being that her methodology was not scientific, not sufficiently detached—but many say it allowed for Goodall's uncommon success with the animals. She was able to get much closer to the chimps than other scientists had before her. Within time the chimps, David Greybeard in particular, began to observe *her*.

But Goodall and van Lawick wanted to get even closer to the chimps, both for better photographs and to better understand the animals' lives. They soon discovered a way to entice the chimps out of their hiding places in the forest. This started accidentally, when some bananas were left out in the camp one day; David Greybeard walked fearlessly into camp, took one, and promptly ran away. After that, Goodall discovered that if she offered David a banana he would bravely accept it. Goodall and van Lawick started leaving bananas out and studying the results. The chimps responded to the appeal, and soon they were coming into the camp frequently. Goodall and van Lawick worked to find a way to limit the number of bananas offered, and a cage was ready to protect them if the chimps should become aggressive at the camp. The work allowed Goodall to observe the chimps daily and get to know them personally.

Goodall's confidence and excitement in the project continued to grow. She started talking about setting up a permanent observation camp at Gombe, and her reports from the wild were gaining respect among other scientists. And Goodall was thriving personally, too. By the time of her return to Cambridge for her third term, in December of 1963, she and van Lawick were madly in love. Their separation that Christmas spurred them to consider marriage. On the day after Christmas, he sent a telegram: "WILL YOU MARRY ME LOVE STOP HUGO." (*Blood*, 270) She accepted the proposal, and in February of 1964 her time in England became busier even than usual as she finished her studies at Cambridge, traveled to Washington, D.C. to present her research at the National Geographic Society, and prepared for the wedding. The celebration was held on March 28, 1964 in London's historic Chelsea Old Church. The entire church was decorated in yellow and white—daffodils and lilies, with Goodall

In 1962, Baron Hugo van Lawick (behind the camera), a photographer sent by *National Geographic*, arrived at Gombe to take pictures for one of Goodall's articles. He intended specifically to record the chimps eating meat and using tools, but van Lawick eventually became Goodall's husband and her partner in observing the chimps at Gombe.

in white and her bridesmaids in yellow and white.

Even in the midst of a traditional wedding, Africa and the chimpanzees were never far from Goodall's mind. The wedding cake was topped with a clay model of David Greybeard, and the reception hall was decorated with large photos of several Gombe chimps, including Goliath, Flo, and Fifi. Louis

Leakey was not able to attend the wedding, but he sent his congratulatory wishes by tape recording. And at the wedding, a congratulatory telegram from the National Geographic Society proudly announced that Goodall, now known officially as Baroness van Lawick-Goodall, had won her second Franklin Burr Award for Contribution to Science, which included an honorarium of $1,500. The chimps preempted the honeymoon, too, for within three days of the wedding, on hearing that Flo had just given birth, the newlyweds raced back to Africa.

Goodall writes in *In the Shadow of Man* that, from a professional point of view, the most exciting thing to happen in 1964 was the birth of Flo's son, Flint. They were able to record on paper and film the weekly development of the wild chimpanzee infant—something that had never been done before. In September of that year, the chimp Melissa gave birth again. The newborn was named Goodall until it was discovered that she was actually a male—and then the infant's name was changed to Goblin. In October, a third infant was born to the chimp Mandy. This one, too, was named Goodall, and this time the name stuck.

Other excitement awaited the newlyweds upon their return to Africa, of a less joyous variety. The banana provisioning was now out of control, with too many new chimps wandering into the camp for safety. Van Lawick had ordered the construction of steel banana boxes in February of that year that would deliver a limited number of bananas by remote control, but the boxes had not yet arrived. So Goodall, van Lawick, and the growing staff decided to move the feeding area up into the valley, farther away from the main camp. This seemed to help the situation tremendously: the scientists could still make their observations, but without disturbing the work and life of those at the base camp.

The couple's own tent was moved up the valley to the feeding area as well, giving the newlyweds some privacy and even a sense of seclusion. But this didn't last for long: a new tent became an office during the day and hosted a research assistant at night. Still, Goodall's letters show a happiness that summer in the simple pleasures of domestic life with her new husband—the fun of a new coffee percolator, the details of their little camp.

GOODALL'S WORK GAINS MOMENTUM

In addition to a growing staff—more research assistants came to work at the camp in that year—the scientists at Gombe also welcomed many visitors during this time. Among them were officials from the National Geographic Society, the governor general of Kenya, and two European researchers. Goodall writes that she was flattered by the positive interest and support of the two researchers and began to appreciate the significance of her work. The growing interest supported Goodall and van Lawick's own plans for a permanent research institute at Gombe. In March of 1964, Goodall mentioned their plans to a committee from the National Geographic Society, and the visiting researchers from Europe were impressed with her work and supported the idea. Louis Leakey endorsed the proposal for National Geographic funds to be used to buy and install some prefabricated, semi-permanent buildings. By December of 1964, the foundations had been laid for these buildings and the proposal was on its way to becoming a reality.

In *Shadow*, Goodall writes that when she first arrived on the sandy beach of the Gombe Stream Chimpanzee Reserve, she never dreamed she was taking the initial step toward the creation of the Gombe Stream Research Centre. She could not have imagined, she writes, that nine years later there would be ten or more students studying the different aspects of chimp behavior as well as observing baboons and red colobus monkeys. But her stature in the scientific community continued to grow and her reputation outside of the academic world also started to gain recognition—largely because of the *National*

Goodall and her husband expanded the research center at Gombe to include the records of multiple research assistants; buildings were erected, and the institute became more established. With the solidification of the institute at Gombe, the *National Geographic* article, her formal training in Cambridge's doctoral program, and her ongoing field research, Goodall built a strong reputation as a scientist.

Geographic article of 1963. By 1966, Dr. Leonard Carmichael, the chairman of the National Geographic Society's Committee for Research and Exploration, said Goodall was "probably the best qualified person in the world today to speak on the subject of chimpanzee behavior in the wild." (*Blood*, 334) Goodall was well on her way to "coming of age" professionally.

And her dreams didn't stop with the permanent research center. By this time, Goodall was talking of establishing a series of chimp reserves all over West Africa, while still fully intending to continue the research at Gombe for the long term. But already the latter part of that dream had become difficult to realize. As she grew in prominence in the field of chimpanzee study, she was called away more and more often from Gombe. She later said it was a withdrawal she regretted. "Yet there were times," she writes, "when I thought back to my early days at Gombe with real nostalgia. . . . But change had been inevitable: there was no way in the world that one person, no matter how dedicated, could have made a really comprehensive study of the Gombe chimpanzees. Hence the research centre." (*Through a Window*, 26)

The first permanent buildings to be built at Gombe—two prefabricated aluminum buildings and a smaller hut for the storage of bananas—were installed by March of 1965. By 1966, they were furnished, painted, regularly used, and even named. The larger of the two units, which included a main office and two smaller rooms where researchers slept, was called Pan Palace; this was a double play on words, as *Pan* is half of the scientific name of the chimpanzee and the building itself resembled an aluminum pan. The smaller building consisted of just a single room and was used as Goodall and van Lawick's sleeping quarters; it was named Lawick Lodge. By May of 1966, a third, semipermanent building was being planned at the beach. This building would serve as a dining hall for the research staff and was named Troglodytes Tavern.

Goodall and van Lawick had to be away from Gombe, and each other, during much of this period of growth between March of 1965 and May of 1966. *National Geographic* had given van Lawick the funding he needed to photograph animals in East Africa. Goodall returned to Cambridge, where she finished writing her doctoral dissertation. Her advisor, Robert Hinde, had serious concerns about her research: like many of his colleagues, he believed it was a mistake to name the subjects as though they were human and that her records should not report the chimps' behavior in a narrative form. Goodall recalls the environment: "When I got to Cambridge University . . . I was greeted with hostility. I'd given the chimpanzees names instead of numbers. I'd dared to talk about them having personalities, their ability to reason and the fact they had emotions. These were cardinal sins."

PAN TROGLODYTES SCHWEINFURTHII

Taxonomy is the system that scientists use to make sense of the many life forms that live or have lived in the Earth's biosphere. Living things are grouped into *taxa* (sing. *taxon*), categories that can include millions of creatures or only one. Grouping is first by kingdom (there are five) and then by, in decreasing order of size, *phylum* (pl. *phyla*) or *division*; *class*; *order* or *subclass*; *family*; *genus* (pl. *genera*); and *species*. (Subcategories are added when necessary to describe evolutionary distinctions, and there *is* some variation in the system.) The more closely interrelated two beings are, the more classifications they will have in common. Humans and chimpanzees both are primates; we are of the same kingdom, phylum, subphylum, class, and order as they but diverge from them at the family level. Chimps (*Pan troglodytes*) are classified as follows:

Kingdom *Animalia* (all animals) or *Metazoa* (all organisms composed of multiple cells)

Phylum *Chordata* (all metazoans that express a certain characteristic before birth)

Subphylum *Vertebrata* (all chordates that develop a backbone)

Class *Mammalia* (all warm-blooded vertebrates with fur and milk-secreting mammary glands)

Order *Primata* (11 families, including humans and all apes)

Family *Pongidae* (all great apes, including gorillas, chimpanzees, bonobos ["pygmy chimps"], and orangutans)

Genus *Pan* (chimps and bonobos)

Species *troglodytes* (chimps only)

Subspecies *verus* (the western subspecies)

Subspecies *troglodytes* (the central subspecies)

Subspecies *schweinfurthii* (the eastern subspecies, the one that Dr. Goodall has studied)

At the same time, Goodall was juggling the demands of her professional success. She worked on a second article for *National Geographic*, finished a draft of her first non-scientific book, delivered a lecture at a prestigious conference in Vienna, and, after a brief return to Gombe, traveled back to Cambridge for oral exams and lectures—this time not *listening* to the lectures, but *giving* them. The lectures were part of a tour of the United States, where Goodall was gaining popularity owing to the publication of her second chimpanzee article in *National Geographic* and a CBS television special called *Miss Goodall and the Wild Chimpanzees*.

THE SERENGETI PLAIN AND A POLIO EPIDEMIC

Professor Hinde approved Goodall's doctoral thesis despite his doubts and her refusal to abandon her naming system, and in May of 1966 she returned to Gombe, thrilled to be reunited with her husband and to resume her studies. During her absence, two new infant chimps had been born, and her namesake, the young chimp Goodall, had died early in February. After a few weeks spent reacquainting herself with the compound and learning the latest news, Goodall set out once more. This time, she headed off to Serengeti Park on a photographic safari with van Lawick, his brother, and two African assistants. The trip took them south to the Serengeti Plain, a region of 15,000 square miles that includes Ngorongoro Crater, Olduvai Gorge, and Tanzania's 5,000−square mile Serengeti National Park. Originally, the group planned to end up at the crater, but they ended up in the park, where they set up a base camp and began their work.

According to *Beyond Innocence*, which tells of Goodall's later years in Africa, she and van Lawick made an important scientific discovery during their time in the Serengeti. After a grass fire burned across the plains, the group drove out and saw a swarm of birds surrounding an ostrich nest in which 20 eggs had been laid. About six eggs were unbroken when the group arrived, and three white Egyptian vultures were able to break these open by picking up, carrying, and throwing stones at the eggs using their beaks. This was another example of wild animals using objects as tools, something that had never been witnessed in the wild before Goodall's observations. Goodall would write of this experience later, first for the magazine *Nature* and then for *National Geographic.*

At Gombe, however, there was not much to celebrate. In the second half of 1966, a polio epidemic had spread from people to the chimpanzees living inside the Gombe Stream Reserve. Goodall had learned of the birth of an infant chimp to Olly, and saw the baby, named Grosvenor, in late August. Although she was initially delighted by the birth—as she was for all new infant chimps to be born at Gombe—a few weeks later Goodall and the researchers noticed that Grosvenor was quite ill. The baby soon became paralyzed and then died. Shortly after that, Goodall and van Lawick had to leave again for another safari, this time traveling north to the national parks of Uganda. When they returned to Gombe in early November of 1966, they learned that a polio epidemic was spreading with full force. There were also reports of humans contracting polio in the villages south and east of the reserve. Louis Leakey arranged to have polio vaccine flown in for all the researchers and chimps, and by January of 1967 the epidemic seemed to have abated. Goodall writes in *Shadow* that those months during the polio epidemic were among the darkest days she had ever lived. Every time a chimp stopped coming to the feeding area, she writes, the researchers started to wonder if they would ever see that chimp again—or if they did, whether he or she would be terribly crippled. In the end, nine chimps were affected by the outbreak; five were paralyzed, and another four died.

Goodall and van Lawick continued their work even through this difficult period. In December of 1966, Goodall had her first encounter with another of Louis Leakey's

The Gombe chimps, who were shy at first, eventually became so comfortable with Goodall that they often wandered into her camp. Watching them daily, she became engrossed in their lives, and she came to mourn those who died. Several chimps died in a polio outbreak in the late 1960s, when Goodall was traveling through Gombe, the Serengeti, and Nairobi; she remembers this as among the worst disasters ever to befall the camp. Here, Goodall visits chimps in an orphan sanctuary she established in Kenya.

primate-study protégés, 34-year-old Dian Fossey, who was on her way to the Congo to begin her work with the mountain gorillas of the Virunga Mountains. Dr. Leakey had arranged for Fossey to spend Christmas with Goodall at Gombe, for he felt Goodall's experience in setting up and maintaining a research camp in the rain forest might be of use to the very inexperienced Fossey. The meeting was not quite a success: Fossey struck the veteran Goodall as far too idealistic. In a letter to her mother, written a few weeks after their encounter, Goodall expressed some skepticism about Dr. Leakey's "gorilla girl":

> She seems to have the most romantic ideas in her head. She keeps saying the meadow is like an alpine meadow. She is determined to get a cow up there, and lots of hens. She will have a bell around the cow's neck. . . . She plans to make bramble jam out of the wild black-berries. Well, when I began with the chimps, I had romantic notions, too. . . . Next we found out that she had not even read [George Schaller's] book carefully. Nor has she during the past three years since she planned to study gorillas, bothered to learn anything about primates. . . . However, let us hope for the best.
>
> (*Beyond Innocence*, 31–32)

Goodall and van Lawick spent much of early 1967 traveling through Gombe, the Serengeti, and Nairobi. Their camp at Gombe had many visitors during this period, including the more than a dozen American and European researchers who came, associates and family members in tow, to live at the chimp reserve. In February of that year, the couple decided to buy a house in a town called Limuru, a suburb of Nairobi about 18 miles outside the center of the city. The couple's son, Hugo Eric Louis van Lawick, was born on March 4. Parenting would prove to be a welcome new challenge for Goodall—and an adventure she would find just as satisfying as her work with the chimpanzees of Gombe.

5

Dr. Goodall as Mother and Wife: 1967–1975

GRUB

Hugo Eric Louis was named for three important men in his life: his father, his great-uncle, and his "foster grandfather"— Louis Leakey.

Goodall writes in *My Life with the Chimpanzees* that the Africans said her son should have been named Simba, after the Swahili word for lion; this was because of some events that took place just three weeks before little Hugo's birth, while Goodall and van Lawick were camping in Ngorongoro Crater. The crater is located inside a long dormant volcano, and now is home to about 100 square miles of grassland, a lake, and a few rivers. Goodall calls it one of the most beautiful places in the world. It is also a place that is famous for its wild animals, especially its black-maned lions.

One night, as Goodall and van Lawick were waiting for dinner, they heard an outburst of shouts. That noise was

Although death was a natural part of a chimp's life cycle that Goodall had to accept, the birth of baby chimps was always a happy event for her. She witnessed the chimps' maternal and protective behavior toward their young all the time—shown here are Judy and her son Oscar, of the Sweetwaters sanctuary in Kenya—but she wasn't able to understand it fully until she had a child of her own.

followed by the banging and clanging of pots and pans. Next came utter silence, followed by the sound of canvas ripping, followed by more shouting and banging. Van Lawick investigated and then rushed back to the tent; he told Goodall that there was a lion outside, between the tent and their car, an SUV. As Goodall explains, the practice in the bush country of Africa is to park one's car near one's tent in case of danger; so the lion was very close. It had already ripped open one tent.

The couple then heard people running to the car—their colleagues had made it to safety. Van Lawick peeked out again, and this time didn't see the lion. He ran to the car, clambered in, and slammed the door; he inched the car closer to the tent, and then Goodall, too, safely made it inside. The couple's colleagues said they had seen three lions—and after turning on their headlights, they saw the three young males. Van Lawick tried to use the car to herd them away from the camp, but, at least at first, they did not want to go. Eventually, they wandered off into the bush, and the group made it safely back to camp. The tents had been damaged, however, so the foursome repaired to a nearby cabin that they knew was empty—only to find a very large, black-maned lion sitting proudly on the front porch. Behind the cabin, a lioness was enjoying a newly killed antelope. In time, the male lion left, and the group was able to enter the cabin without disturbing the female.

"No wonder they thought that my son, born so soon afterward, should have been called Simba!" Goodall writes. "As it was, he became known as Grub to his family and closest friends. There was no very good reason for this." (*My Life*, 80) Goodall came from a family where nicknames or all sorts were given to just about everyone. When Grub was just a baby, Goodall and van Lawick were studying hyenas in Ngorongoro Crater. Hyenas are skilled hunters who can chase down wildebeests and zebras. They are like chimps in some ways—particularly in that they travel together in small groups of friendly individuals. In addition, hyenas have distinct personalities and behavior, and they are territorial, too, sometimes killing hyenas from other groups. The main difference between the social behavior of chimps and that of hyenas is that females are dominant among hyenas, and males among chimps.

Grub spent a good portion of his early years on the Serengeti, according to Goodall's book *Reason for Hope*, while van Lawick made films of the hyenas, lions, and wild dogs. But he spent the most time at Gombe, where Goodall continued to oversee her study of the chimpanzees. Even as her work brought her closer to them, she had to work to keep the chimps away from her son, for they were hunters and liked best to prey on other primates. To wild chimps, there is no meaningful difference between an infant human and an infant monkey. Before Grub came along, Goodall and van Lawick had heard of two instances in which human babies were killed for food in the Gombe area. They didn't want to take any chances with their beloved son, so before he learned to walk, Grub would sometimes stay in a large blue cage to protect from him chimps and other wild animals, including the often aggressive baboons.

THE EFFECT OF MOTHERHOOD ON THE WORK

As a result of this concern and her new role as mother (in addition to scholar and scientist), Goodall's approach to her work changed. She could no longer follow the chimps into the forest, so she relied on her students and staff to do that, and the result was a feeling of distance from the students and their work. Still, as the recalls in *Reason for Hope*, she was willing to make the sacrifice:

> I merely administered the research stations and spent time being a mother. There were times when I felt a deep sadness and sense of loss for those days when I roamed the forests, alone with the chimpanzees. Now, it seemed, there was a student keenly interested in every single individual chimpanzee as part of a particular aspect of behavior he or she was studying. Which was wonderful in a way, only it meant that I felt something of an interloper. However, I discovered every day anew that having my own child more than made up for that.
>
> (87)

Goodall admits that she sometimes looks back on this time with a bit of regret. It was not that she didn't love her son or enjoy being a mother. It was more selfish than that, she writes: the regret came from knowing that she could never have collected on her own even a small portion of all the interesting information the students and staff were collecting in the field during this time.

Trying to juggle career and motherhood was not easy, but in the end Goodall settled into a routine. She usually spent the mornings at the house at Gombe working on scientific papers for publication and proposals for research grants. Grub would play on the beach during this time, a member of the staff always keeping a close eye on him. At some point in each day, Goodall would go to the feeding station, where the bananas were distributed, in the hope of glimpsing some of her research subjects. She spent the afternoons with her son.

Goodall learned a great deal from watching the chimpanzees' behavior toward their young, and she tried to apply some of these lessons to her relationship with Grub. In particular, she learned that having an infant should be fun: in the afternoons, she and Grub would just play, for hours. They spent a good deal of time at Lake Tanganyika, and Grub very quickly became a skillful swimmer. Goodall said that being with a child makes it possible to see the world through the eyes of a child—and that this was an important lesson for her to learn. Every day, she said, she understood more of the meaning of her life—because she could witness all of it through the eyes of her son. Goodall writes nostalgically that she considers the experiences of these years among the most significant in her life.

During this time when Grub was young, Goodall also became interested again in the "nature versus nurture" debate—that is, whether human behaviors are determined by genetic makeup (one's "nature," or what one is "born to be") or by learned patterns (nurture, or what one is *taught* to be). This debate has died down in recent years, Goodall writes, as most have come to believe that both family history *and* environment influence the development of children—but it was still being

Hugo Eric Louis van Lawick, known as Grub, was born to Goodall and Hugo van Lawick in 1967. Goodall loved parenting, but having a child meant scaling back her work at Gombe. She left the observation and other fieldwork more and more to the other researchers. This photograph was taken in 1974.

discussed passionately when Grub was a baby.

When she had questions about being a mother, Goodall said she had two sources of advice. The first was traditional—the teachings of popular experts such as Dr. Benjamin Spock, who wrote a famous book on childrearing that has helped many parents through difficult times. But she also looked to the chimps, and to one mother, Flo, in particular. From watching Flo and the other chimps with their children, Goodall learned that "a secure childhood was likely to lead to self-reliance and independence in adulthood" and that "a disturbed early life might well result in an insecure adult." (*Reason*, 88)

The most important thing, Goodall writes, was the character of the mother. Mothers who behaved toward their offspring as Flo did toward hers—that is to say, who were playful, affectionate, tolerant, and supportive—seemed to raise chimps who had good relationships with the community once they became adults. Those mothers who were like the chimp Passion—more strict, less playful, and less nurturing—seemed to raise young who were tense and uncomfortable as adults. This trend seemed to play out with daughters in particular, but the sons were influenced as well. Specifically, Goodall writes, those mother chimps who, like Flo, had relaxed relationships with other adults, and who were assertive and confident, gave their children a better start in life than the mother chimps who were timid and whose relationships with other adults were tense.

Goodall writes that under the aegis of Dr. Spock, Flo, her

COULD A CHIMP POSE A THREAT TO A HUMAN BABY?

. . . [W]hen Grub was small, we had to be very careful [at Gombe]. Chimpanzees . . . are hunters. I knew that many years before I had arrived at Gombe, chimpanzees had taken two African babies for food. Of course, that seems shocking to us. But from the chimps' point of view it is no different to take a human baby than a baboon baby.

—*My Life with the Chimpanzees*

own mother, and Mother Nature, Grub got off to a good start in life. During his first three years, mother and son were never apart—not even for a night. She devoted at least half of each day to him. Once he reached an age to begin schooling, Goodall tried to teach him herself; but this was not a viable arrangement, so she looked to correspondence courses for his education. The family finally arranged to have young people who wanted a year of adventure and travel between high school and college to come to Gombe to be Grub's tutors—and have the thrill of living in Africa. When Grub was sent to school in England when he was a little older, he lived with Goodall's mother; he was already well familiar with The Birches, as that is where the family had stayed every time they'd left Africa. He considered The Birches an extension of his African home.

"There is no doubt," Goodall writes, "that my observations of the chimpanzees helped me to be a better mother. . . . I found that the experience of being a mother helped me better understand chimpanzee maternal behavior: it is hard to empathize with or understand emotions we ourselves have not experienced." (*Reason*, 90) For example, Goodall says, she never really understood the basic, powerful instinct of "mother-love" until she had Grub. Once she was a mother, she learned that if something frightened her son, or threatened him, she would feel angry. "How much more easily I could now understand the feelings of a chimpanzee mother who furiously waved her arms and barked out threats to any who approached her infant too closely, or at a playmate who inadvertently hurt her child." (*Reason*, 90)

DIVORCE AND REMARRIAGE

Goodall achieved several important scientific goals during this period. In 1970, she finished the book *Grub: The Bush Baby*. A year later, in addition to taking a teaching position at Stanford University, Goodall also saw the publication of her well-received book *In the Shadow of Man*, which chronicled the first ten years of research at Gombe and the discoveries she had made

Goodall learned from the maternal habits of the chimps that having a child should be enjoyable. The mother chimps who were playful and supportive, she noticed, tended to raise confident offspring, whereas those young who were raised without open affection never seemed to fit in well as adults. Yoshi and her son Toshi, shown in this image, are from the Los Angeles Zoo.

during that time. Her work at Gombe continued to thrive and expand, with more and more students and scholars coming to study and learn.

But while her relationship with her son thrived, her relationship with her husband began to fall apart. Van Lawick's work in photography and film-making took him all over the world, but Goodall felt the need to be at Gombe most of the time. Also, as a visiting professor of psychiatry and human biology, she had to spend time at Stanford, too. They had little time together, or to be a family. In addition, Goodall writes, the couple was incompatible in many areas. She says that they had known about these differences in point of view at the time of their marriage but had felt and hoped that the tension would erode with time. This didn't happen, and their fighting became more frequent. By 1974, when Grub was seven years old, the couple separated; then they were divorced. They remained good friends over the years, she writes, "but it was all very sad, especially for Grub, for he, of course, loved us both." (*Reason*, 92)

In fact, she'd already met the man who would become her next husband. Derek Bryceson, injured in a World War II plane crash at the age of 19, had been told when that he would never walk again, and he'd decided to prove the doctors wrong. After teaching himself to walk again with the help of a cane, he'd earned a degree in agriculture from Cambridge, Goodall's alma mater. He'd then been offered farming work in England, work he called "suitable for an invalid" (*Reason*, 98) —and instead had gone to Kenya, where he'd worked as a farmer for two years. After that, he'd applied successfully to the British government for a job working a wheat farm at the foot of Mount Kilimanjaro. Two years later, he'd met a local political leader and agreed to start working toward Tanzanian independence from Britain; he was the only white Member of Parliament when Tanzania *did* gain its independence, and he had been an important political figure in Tanzania ever since.

Goodall had first met the tall, slim, white-haired Bryceson in 1967, when he'd come to Gombe as the Minister of Agriculture. When she met him again in 1973, he was Tanzania's new Director of National Parks, and this time he was more attentive to her. He was graceful and confident despite his injury. "[Bryceson had] a strong and forceful character; he was honest to the point of brutality; and he had a wonderful sense of humor," Goodall writes in *Reason for Hope*. "He was also an idealist with the will and energy to work for positive change." (97)

A TRAGEDY NARROWLY AVERTED

This second relationship came into being rather more intensely than the first had done; the bond between Goodall and Bryceson was forged in circumstances of the most extreme kind.

To get around Africa, Bryceson would fly his four-seated Cessna, and sometimes Goodall and Grub would join him. Shortly after Goodall and Bryceson became reacquainted, the three of them and a pilot decided to fly to the Ruaha National Park. They had been in the air almost an hour when they noticed a small plume of smoke coming from under the instrument panel—similar, they recall, to the smoke made by a cigarette that has been not fully stubbed out in an ashtray. They still had 45 more minutes to fly before they reached the park, and rugged, rocky terrain stretched below them, covered with trees. As they flew on, Bryceson checked the instruments and everything seemed fine—with the exception of the smoke. Goodall says they tried their best to ignore the smoke, and simply prayed as they flew toward their destination. Those 45 minutes, Goodall remembers, seemed to last a lifetime.

In time, they made it to the park and saw the little airstrip near the ranger camp and rest house. They had been lucky—there were still no flames coming from the smoke. But as they made their first approach landing, a herd of zebras crossed the runway. The pilot pulled the plane's nose up quickly to avoid crashing into the zebras—and then, just as suddenly, he lost his nerve and decided to make an emergency landing. "I was fussing with Grub's seat belt," Goodall writes, "when I heard Derek say, urgently, 'You're not trying to land here, are you? Don't!' The last word was a shout—but it was too late." (*Reason*, 99) By this time, the plane was flying at twice its normal speed for a landing. It hit the ground. One of the wings caught a tree and swung the plane around, keeping it from flipping over and bursting into flames; utterly out of control, the plane continued to barrel through the bush.

The African sunset. It was in just such an atmosphere that Derek Bryceson proposed marriage to Goodall after their near-fatal plane crash. Bryceson, Goodall's second husband, would become a great source of strength to her for the five years of their marriage.

When at last the craft had come to a stop, the pilot then opened his door and shouted for everyone to get out quickly because the plane was going up in flames. He abandoned his passengers and left the engine running. Goodall urged Grub to get out and follow the pilot. He did just as he was told, and when he'd reached a safe distance away from the plane, he turned to a frightening sight: the luggage had fallen around Bryceson, so the door on his side wouldn't open more than a few inches, and Bryceson was having serious trouble in escaping the plane. Somehow, he was able to pull himself up and out of the other door, just as the park staff arrived. In time, Goodall and Bryceson also made it out of the plane, and the park staff was amazed to see that everyone was alive.

Exhausted and frightened though they were, the group then had to wade back across the Ruaha River—even though large crocodiles were often seen cruising this waterway. But, Goodall writes, Grub assured the group that if God had saved them when the plane had crashed, He wouldn't let them be eaten by the crocodiles. So they crossed—without seeing one crocodile—and made it to the park house. Once they were safe,

BECOME A PRIMATOLOGIST

Primatologists, researchers devoted to the study of primates, represent a diverse group of conservationists, scientists, educators, veterinarians, and medical researchers; of course, many educational paths can make this career a possibility. The American Society of Primatologists reports that most who enter the field have backgrounds in biology/zoology, psychology, anthropology, or veterinary science. The most appropriate courses of undergraduate training, though, are those in science education, ecology and conservation, biology, journalism or scientific writing, molecular biology, animal behavior, virology, paleontology, geology, natural-resource management, or even statistics and computer science. Advanced degrees may be required, depending on the type of position the candidate wishes to find, from universities offering courses in those fields or from medical or veterinary schools. Most important are a background in biology and excellent communication skills; a knowledge of statistics helps, too, in research like Dr. Goodall's. Essential is a love of, and respect for, the animals.

refreshed, and drinking hot tea, Goodall writes, the shock of the crash began to hit her:

> I had been sure, as the plane slammed into the ground and careered among the trees, that we were about to die. I remember thinking to myself, 'This plane is going to crash and burst into flames.' Yet I had felt no fear whatever during the crash itself. None at all. I think the reflective part of my mind went numb.
>
> (*Reason*, 100–101)

It was a defining moment for both Goodall and Bryceson. When the evening had come and the air was cooler, they drove into the park; elephants were drinking there, framed by the warm orange-red of the setting sun. Goodall and Bryceson were relieved at simply being alive—and well aware of the impermanence of life. Africa had never seemed more beautiful. Bryceson asked Goodall to marry him—and she agreed.

6

A Time of Great Hardship: 1975–1981

Why do my helpers and I continue to observe the chimpanzees at Gombe after nearly two decades? Partly because chimpanzees are fascinating creatures with advanced brains and complex behavior.
—**Jane Goodall, "Life and Death at Gombe" (1979)**

A KIDNAPPING THREATENS THE PROJECT

Goodall and Bryceson were married by February of 1975. They often still lived apart, for Bryceson lived in Dar es Salaam, Tanzania's capital city, and his work took him all over the country. Goodall's work kept her at Gombe when she was not teaching at Stanford or lecturing around the world. By this time, dozens of students, too, had come to Gombe, to undertake their own research on chimpanzees and baboons.

Then, in May of 1975, an incident took place at Gombe that may well be its most terrifying. According to Goodall's book *Reason for Hope*, one night, 40 armed men crossed Lake

Lake Tanganyika. Armed raiders crossed this lake and kidnapped four researchers from Goodall's camp. Although the researchers were eventually released, all non-Tanzanians were ordered to leave the area due to the region's chronic political turmoil, and the work at Gombe was carried on temporarily by Tanzanian field staff. Goodall credits Derek Bryceson, an important figure in Tanzanian politics, with continuing the work under such trying conditions.

Tanganyika from Zaire (now known as Congo) and raided the camp. The shouting woke the park warden, who investigated and was captured. The raiders held a rifle to her head and ordered her to take them to the student houses. She refused, but by that time the raiders had found four students — the number they had hoped to capture, as they had prepared two huts with two mattresses each on the other side of the lake. Satisfied with the students they had kidnapped, the raiders released the park warden, and they took the students, three American and one Dutch, in a boat back across the lake. Someone reported hearing four gunshots as the boats floated away, and everyone at the camp worried the students had been killed. They would not know for many weeks what had become of their colleagues.

The political turmoil in the region at that time was such that everyone who was not from Tanzania was ordered to leave Gombe. Goodall and Grub moved to Bryceson's home in Dar es Salaam and worried constantly. At last, about two weeks later, one of the students was released with a ransom demand. The other three were alive—at least at that time. But, as Goodall writes in *Reason for Hope*, the ransom not only asked for large amounts of money and the shipment of arms, but the raiders also made demands of the government that Bryceson knew could not or would not be met. Eventually, the ransom was paid; the money would be used to support a revolutionary movement that, 20 years later, would topple the government, take over Zaire, and rename the country the Democratic Republic of the Congo. At the last minute, though, the raiders changed their minds, and sent over only two of the three remaining hostages. Goodall worried the men would kill the last student to make a statement. But for some reason, after several more weeks, the rebels sent the fourth kidnapped student back across the lake. The four were physically unharmed, but all had suffered a terrible ordeal.

Without Bryceson, Goodall writes, the kidnapping probably would have meant the end of the work at Gombe. But Bryceson helped with the administration of the research center and supporting the Tanzanian field staff, who took on more research duties once the foreign students and scholars left. He also was a nationalized Tanzanian and knew Swahili as well as English. He was respected in political circles and helped build up the research center, which for years relied solely on observations made by the Tanzanian field staff.

Despite the help from Bryceson, the years following the kidnapping were a struggle for Goodall. First, her employment with Stanford was not renewed. Then several organizations that had provided grants the studies at Gombe decided no longer to fund the research, and Goodall was left to raise money by lecturing in the United States. In 1977, with the help of Princess Genevieve di San Faustino, she established a nonprofit, tax-exempt organization called the Jane Goodall Institute for Wildlife Research, Education, and Conservation; this would eventually become Goodall's primary means of raising money to finance her work.

WHAT BECAME OF LAURENT KABILA?

Laurent Kabila, the leader of the African rebels who kidnapped Goodall's students, ousted Zaire dictator Mobutu Sese Seko in May of 1997 and, amid the cheers of the crowd, renamed the nation the Democratic Republic of the Congo. The four kidnapped students—Carrie Hunter, Stephen Smith, Barbara Smuts, and Emilie Bergman—have since broken their 22-year silence, determined to expose Kabila's past as a terrorist. Their work has gained the support of U.S. Congresswoman Lynn Rivers of Michigan and the ear of the State Department; but the U.S. government, which once supported Mobutu and to which the students have applied for assistance, has an interest in the economic stability it believes Kabila's government will bring to the region. Kabila has been under great pressure to change his tactics, and Secretary of State Madeline Albright initially praised Kabila's "strong start" and "positive steps" toward reducing human-rights abuses; but Kabila's old methods continued.

Despite these troubles, Goodall's domestic life was very happy during this period. She and Bryceson grew ever closer. In 1976, when Grub turned nine years old, he went to England to live with Goodall's mother and attend an English school nearby. The child who had been raised in Africa was now settled comfortably in England. He even slept in the same room that Goodall had occupied from the age of twelve. Mother and son spent every holiday and school break together—except for those times when he visited his father, Hugo van Lawick. While they were apart, Goodall writes many letters to Grub, giving him updates of news that particularly interested him— especially how the fish and dogs were doing without him. The fish were kept at the house in Dar es Salaam in an aquarium, and Bryceson would often add seashells that he had collected to the display. The dogs included Beetle, a miniature golden retriever named Spider, and then Spider's daughter, Wagga.

"THE PEACE THAT PASSETH UNDERSTANDING"

Both Spider and Wagga died in a canine virus epidemic in May of 1980. That sadness, however real, did nothing to get Goodall ready for the news that Bryceson had been stricken suddenly with a terrible illness. It started in September of 1979. Bryceson had been suffering from severe stomach pains and eventually went to see a doctor in Dar es Salaam, and when he left for the appointment Goodall suddenly knew what the diagnosis would be. When he returned, he told her the doctors had found an "abdominal mass"—likely cancer. Within a week, the couple flew to England to see one of the best surgeons in the country. After examining Bryceson and carrying out many tests, the doctor was hopeful: he said Bryceson had a tumor in his colon that could be removed with a simple operation. Many patients had made a full recovery, the doctor said, and Goodall and Bryceson had nothing to worry about.

When Bryceson was rolled away for his surgery, the doctors again told her not to worry—and asked her to return in three hours. She spent this time walking the streets of London, and when she returned the nurses said the operation would take a little longer than expected. Several hours later, Bryceson was rolled out of the operating room; a doctor asked to speak to Goodall alone. He told her he had been mistaken—that Bryceson's case was hopeless. The cancer had spread throughout his body, and he probably had only three months more to live. Goodall has said that after that doctor's departure she felt more alone than ever before.

As the reality started to sink in, Goodall derived great strength from her mother, who came to see her in London, and together the two decided to try other kinds of healing for Bryceson. So Goodall made appointments with homeopaths and healers throughout the city—they even visited a clinic in Germany—but no one offered her any more hope than the doctor had offered the night after Bryceson's surgery. But somehow they regained hope, and for about two months they believed that Bryceson would live.

Some people have criticized Goodall for having false hope at this time, but she doesn't agree with this criticism at all. During these two months, Goodall writes in *Reason for Hope*, Bryceson was filled with mental energy. He began work on his autobiography, and she typed it up for him. Many friends flew to visit the couple in Germany. And the couple spent much time together, connected in their pursuit of a common goal— his life.

Still, after about two months Bryceson's health began to decline. He was in pain more and more often, and soon needed morphine just to bear it. The last words he spoke were "I didn't know such pain was possible." (*Reason*, 159) On the last day, October 12, 1980, he did not regain consciousness, and in the night, he died. Watching Bryceson's slow death was one of the most challenging times of Goodall's life. "I was with him throughout his last three months," she writes. "Every day. It was the hardest time, the cruelest time, of my life—watching

After Bryceson's death from cancer in 1980, Goodall returned to the healing forest; she found comfort there and in the chimps she had come to know so well. The grieving process was slow, but her experience in Africa helped her through it: "The forest," she says, "and the spiritual power that was so real in it, had given me 'the peace that passeth understanding.'"

someone I love dying slowly, and in pain, from cancer. I had always believed that this was something I simply could not cope with, but when the time came, I had no choice. I had to watch him get weaker, and suffer, and die." (*Reason*, 154)

Goodall briefly returned to her family home, The Birches, after Bryceson's death, and then flew back to Tanzania. Bryceson had asked to be cremated and to have his ashes dispersed into the Indian Ocean, which he had loved and marveled at throughout his life. After that, Goodall returned to Gombe. She writes in *Reason for Hope* that she had hoped to find healing and strength in the old forest, and had hoped that contact with the chimpanzees, who are so accepting of whatever life brings them, would help her deal with her own grief. The first two days there were terribly sad, especially at night when she was alone in the home where they had shared so many happy times. On the third night, though, Goodall dreamed that Bryceson was visiting her. He comforted her and urged her to continue on. When she woke up in the morning, she felt a little happier, and better able to get by.

Gradually, in the forest at Gombe, Goodall began to heal. She again enjoyed time spent with the chimpanzees, and continued to tour the world giving lectures on her work in Africa. During this time, her mother suffered a medical emergency and needed to have a valve replaced in her weak heart. With Bryceson's death so fresh in her memory, she was hesitant to visit her in the hospital but did, in time. The operation was a success. Later, Goodall started work on a project to create the Bryceson scholarship using funds donated by the Tanzania Food and Nutrition Centre after Bryceson's death. He had been named chairman of this group just a few months before his death. In time, the scholarship grew and would eventually be administered by Cornell University. Although the bulk of the work started in 1981, the first Bryceson scholar, Godwin Ndossi, wouldn't be named until 1985.

It took a year from Bryceson's death for Goodall to move beyond her anger, sorrow, and self-pity. The night she reconciled some of her pain, she cried herself to sleep. 'But tears can be healing, and I woke knowing that while I would always grieve Bryceson's passing, and the manner of it, I could cope with my grieving. The forest, and the spiritual power that was so real in it, had given me 'the peace that passeth understanding.'" (*Reason*, 181)

7

The Conservation Message: 1981–2000

Every individual matters. Every individual has a role to play. Every individual makes a difference.
—**Jane Goodall**

CHIMPANZOO, GOMBE, AND
THE CHIMPANZEES OF GOMBE

Goodall slowly returned to her busy routine following Bryceson's death. One of the projects she undertook was ChimpanZoo, which she founded in 1984. The concept for ChimpanZoo came to Goodall while she was on an American lecture tour: to establish a network of zoos and research facilities that together would monitor the behavior and psychology of chimps in captivity. ChimpanZoo became a great success; the sheer number of its subjects, some 130 chimps now, makes it the largest ape study ever conducted. Participating researchers from twelve zoos present their findings and related research

Goodall's affection for her chimpanzees has led her to an abiding concern for the natural world, making her now more a naturalist than a primatologist. Interviewer Claudia Dreifus asked Goodall in 1999 whether she returned to Africa often, and Goodall said she did not: "If I were sitting in the field now . . . I wouldn't be happy . . . [b]ecause I have a mission: organizing to help the environment."

to colleagues and the public at a conference held every year, and the information they collect is published in journals and added to an open online database. The Jane Goodall Institute continues to support the program.

Another project was one that was never far from Goodall's mind or heart—the continuing research at Gombe. The

Seeing chimps kept in uncomfortable cages and otherwise poor conditions upset Goodall to the point of ardent activism, and she established ChimpanZoo in 1984 to study the effects of captivity on chimps. Indeed, her concern for the chimps goes so far that she has been criticized for anthropomorphizing them—treating them too much like humans.

research center grew further during these years, and the staff started videotaping the chimps as part of their studies. Many Americans visited Gombe during this time, as well, including anthropologist Christopher Boehm, who came from the University of Northern Kentucky to study the vocal communication of chimps, and Richard Wrangham, who had studied at Gombe and now was a professor of anthropology at the University of Michigan. Goodall also started working with chimp specialists from Japan. This work would lead later to several important awards, including the Kyoto Prize for Basic

Science, Japan's most prestigious scientific honor, in 1990.

But the most absorbing project of this period was a new book, *The Chimpanzees of Gombe: Patterns of Behavior.* The effort to write it had started in the late 1970s. Initially, Goodall had thought she could produce this book by simply expanding her writings of the late 1960s. But she had forgotten that in the early days she had been working alone or with one person, taking notes and collecting information, and since then dozens of people had started making their own daily observations, resulting in a vast amount of information that would not be as easy to synthesize as Goodall's earlier observations had been. But she undertook the task anyway, with the help of a research assistant. By 1984, she thought she was close to completing the book. It was enormous; according to Goodall's *Beyond Innocence*, the project consisted of 19 chapters, 5 appendixes, 20 pages of references, and 2 indexes—more than 650 over-sized pages in all, in small, encyclopedia-style print, with dozens of detailed maps, charts, and graphs and hundreds of photographs. *The Chimpanzees of Gombe* went to press in 1986, and Goodall was relieved enough to call this development a dream come true. The book appeared in stores in September of that year and received glowing reviews and many awards.

But the most important impact of the book was its place in a major international conference of chimp experts that was sponsored by the Chicago Academy of Sciences and called *Understanding Chimpanzees.* The conference was a crowning moment in Goodall's career, a "great public acknowledgement of her pioneering role, seminal position, and breakthrough achievement in the study of humankind's closest relative." (*Beyond Innocence,* 269) Many notable scientists gathered at this conference, as did some representatives from zoos and laboratories—as long as their work was "noninvasive." By the end of the conference, some important issues had emerged. First, most of the researchers who had worked in the field were discussing how the wild chimps in Africa were being threatened by the environmental destruction and hunted for meat and by collectors who traded them as captive pets. The other important issue to emerge from the conference was the worry about chimps that were kept in captivity—those kept at zoos and labs, as pets, or in the entertainment industry.

About 30 researchers ended the conference by forming an organization to help wild chimpanzees and set standards of care for chimps kept in captivity. The organization was called the Committee for the Conservation and Care of Chimpanzees (CCCC) and was funded by the Jane Goodall Institute but functioned independently. The first president of the organization was Geza Teleki, an American born in Hungary who had been a student at Gombe and later helped establish the first national park in Sierra Leone, West Africa. In time, the committee grew to have a powerful voice in the world of chimpanzees.

The conference would change Goodall's life in other ways. Before she went to Chicago, she was simply a scientist doing her own work and, although renowned, not extraordinarily soughtafter for lectures and public appearances. After the conference and the appearance of her most recent scientific book, her popularity soared. More than ever, people wanted to hear what Goodall had to say.

NEW CAUSES: LABORATORY CONDITIONS
AND THE STATUS OF THE CHIMP

One of the topics on which Goodall was speaking most passionately during these years was that of chimpanzees in laboratories. But although she heard of the dangers to chimps in biomedical research laboratories, she did not witness them herself until 1987.

Her concern for the issue was prompted by a videotape shot in December of 1986 by a group of animal-rights activists who broke into SEMA, a tax-funded research laboratory in Maryland in which some 500 primates—mostly monkeys, but

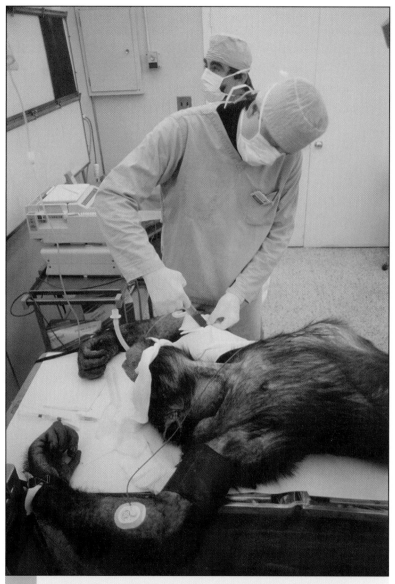

Because chimp DNA is remarkably similar to that of humans, chimps are widely considered good test subjects for research on human diseases. Conditions in the research labs are often deplorable, though, and ever since her visit to SEMA Goodall has spoken out for an end to testing on animals.

some chimpanzees—were being studied for the testing of vaccines. The activists made a videorecording of the conditions in the laboratory and sent that recording to People for the Ethical Treatment of Animals (PETA), who in turn edited the tape into an 18-minute documentary (*Breaking Barriers*) and sent the revision to various people who might be interested. Goodall received her copy of the tape just before Christmas of 1986. According to Peterson, the tape horrified Goodall. "Particularly for someone who had known wild chimpanzees— with all their clearly expressed humanlike emotions and obvious intelligence, their loving family bonds, their individual personalities—the tape conjured up a Dantean sort of world, a nightmare vision that was disturbing indeed." (*Beyond Innocence*, 315)

Goodall asked to see the facility in Maryland, and in March of 1987 her request was granted. The records from the facility show that some 78 primates had died over the previous five years, including 26 monkeys killed by steam from a broken heating pipe. In addition, the lab had been reprimanded by the U.S. Department of Agriculture for violating federal standards of animal care. Among the many problems reported at the lab was that of the chimps' cramped cages, but the worst offense shown in the tape, and later seen in person by Goodall, was the way in which the animals lived. They were taken from a breeding colony when they were 18 months old, and kept in a pair for about six months, in a cage in which they could hardly move. Each "subject" was then injected with a virus—anything from a respiratory virus to a deadly one, such as HIV, which causes AIDS—and separated from his or her companion, enclosed in a small steel box with a window on one side for observation. The apes were kept alone for the duration of the study—sometimes as long as three years. "It might be argued that to subject almost any animal to such extreme isolation and sensory deprivation would amount to simple cruelty," Dale Peterson writes, "but to treat a chimpanzee that way seemed cruel to the point of perversity." Getting through the visit took all of Goodall's courage; even repeated screenings of the video-tape had not prepared her for the reality of the lab. One chimp Goodall saw that day, named Barbie, appeared to be either drugged or completely lost in despair.

Goodall criticized this situation others aggressively. In time, a new person was named to lead the laboratory in Maryland, and he greatly changed the whole physical and social structure of the organization. First, he allowed for large plexiglass cubicles in which the chimps lived in pairs and from which they could see other chimps. In addition, they had toys and "enrichment devices" and human volunteers came to visit and play with the young chimps. But problems still existed at labs around the

BIRTH OF AN ACTIVIST

It would not be stretching the truth to say that Dr. Goodall's visit to the Maryland laboratory began her activism in earnest. She recounts her own reaction best, in *Visions of Caliban*:

Even the repeated viewing of the video did not prepare me for the stark reality of that laboratory. I was ushered by white-coated men who smiled nervously or glowered, into a nightmare world. Outside, everyday life went on as usual, with the sun and the trees and the birds. Inside, where no daylight had ever penetrated, it was dim and colorless. I looked into room after room lined with small, bare cages, stacked one above the other. I watched as monkeys paced around their tiny prisons, making bizarre abnormal movements. . . . [C]himp babies peered out from the semi-darkness of their tiny cells. . . . I am still haunted by their eyes, and the eyes of the other chimps I saw that day. They were dull and blank, like the eyes of people who have lost all hope. . . .

world, and Goodall started to crusade even more vigorously for the ethical treatment of captive chimps.

After visiting the Maryland lab in 1987, Goodall started to speak frankly about the conditions in her lectures and writings. She wrote a powerful editorial for *The New York Times Magazine* in May of 1987 that pointed out that the chimp is more like a human than is any other animal, and that chimps were being treated inhumanely. Although chimps are useful for research because their DNA is so similar to humans, she writes, because they are not fully human, they were being treated as "oversized rats." Although she spoke passionately on the subject, she didn't express radical ideas at first. She didn't debate whether chimps should be used for research in general, and she didn't call for removing them from labs; she just wanted to improve the conditions for those chimps who were *already* living in labs. But she realized later that a new mindset was needed: "Let us stop saying that, while it is unfortunate, some animals will always be needed, and instead admit that the practice is unethical and the sooner we stop doing it the better. Let science direct its collectively awesome intellect toward phasing out all animal research. Human history is full of inspiring stories of those who achieved the impossible." (*Reason*, 221)

Another advocacy position Goodall took during this time was an effort to change the wording in the U.S. Endangered Species Act. The CCCC had petitioned the U.S. Fish and Wildlife Service to upgrade the status of chimpanzees from "threatened" to "endangered," a change that would provide better protection for wild chimps. While the Fish and Wildlife Service reviewed the petition, more than 54,000 postcards, letters and messages were left at the agency's offices in support of the change. Of those comments, more than 40 came from members of African governments and organizations and experts, such as Goodall, who had studied chimps in the field. During this same time, the Fish and Wildlife Service received only six letters citing opposition to the change; one of those letters was from a circus representative, and the other five came from people involved in biomedical research. In the end, Peterson writes in *Beyond Innocence,* the U.S. Fish and Wildlife Service chose a compromise—stating that the chimps were endangered if they lived in a forest in Africa, but threatened if they were kept in a cage outside of Africa.

GARNERING SUPPORT

Goodall continued to support all of her causes through her lectures and serious fundraising on behalf of chimpanzees. This effort was helped greatly by the publication of three important books for adults: *Through a Window: My Thirty Years with the Chimpanzees of Gombe,* which was published in 1990; *Visions of Caliban: On Chimpanzees and People,* co-authored with Dale Peterson and published in 1993; and *Reason for Hope: A Spiritual Journey,* co-authored with the theologian Phillip Berman and published in 1999. In addition, she wrote a popular book for children during this period, *My Life with the Chimpanzees,* which was published in 1988, and a series, *Animal Family.* While writing and promoting these books, she also attended some influential fundraising events, such as a dinner held in May of 1991 for more than 1,000 guests, including Johnny Carson, Jane Fonda, and Jack Lemmon.

Goodall also spent much of her time visiting schools and speaking to children during this time. She started by going to all of the secondary schools in Dar es Salaam to talk of her time and experiences with the chimpanzees at Gombe. These talks grew into an organization for children that Goodall called "Roots and Shoots"—whose mission was "to foster respect and compassion for all living things, to promote understanding of all cultures and beliefs, and to inspire each individual to take action and make the world a better place for animals, the environment, and the human community."

Much of Goodall's current work involves efforts to communicate her love of chimpanzees and the natural world, and in addition to her more scholarly work she has written many books for adults and children. Here she plays with 3-year-old Bahati at a sanctuary in Kenya.

The program's name comes from two of Goodall's favorite plant analogies: roots have a firm foundation, and although shoots are small, they can break apart walls to reach light if they have to. Roots and Shoots began in Tanzania in 1991 and has grown to include several thousand members in dozens of countries around the world. The goal of the program is to get its participants to work toward improving their own communities, at the local level, and each group gets involved in at least one hands-on activity in each of three areas: activities for animals, for people, and for the environment. A letter that

Goodall wrote in June of 1999 to a Roots and Shoots chapter in Virginia, updating the students on her latest trip to Gombe and the most recent film crew to come to Africa to capture images of chimps in the wild, shows a keen interest in her disciples. She relates excitedly that the program is growing:

> Now, in addition to a lot of interest in China & Dubai, I think we've found a way of starting off in Russia— & even in Albania. Anyway I look forward—very much—to hearing what you all do in your Roots & Shoots clubs. The best part of my work is to hear what is going on. All the ideas & plans—and how they are fulfilled. All the ways the world is always being made a better place for all life, for all individuals.
>
> (*Beyond Innocence,* 396)

Goodall received the National Geographic Society's prestigious Hubbard Medal in 1995, awarded "for her extraordinary study of wild chimpanzees and for tirelessly defending the natural world we share," and in that same year she was awarded the honorary rank of Commander of the British Empire (CBE) by Queen Elizabeth II.

In the spring of 2000, to mark the fortieth anniversary of her research at Gombe, Goodall launched a multi-city celebrational tour that she called the Reason for Hope Celebration. The idea behind the tour was not only to raise money to support Goodall's work, but also to spread the word about what she was doing and to inspire communities to get involved.

8

The Present and the Future

Dr. Jane is one of those rare individuals who combine the determination to go after what they want in life until they get it with a desire to make the world a better place. Indeed, it is this desire that has been the object of all her work over the past forty years. A lifetime of working to improve the world is no small achievement, and her legacy has already grown to global proportions.

—**Dr. Oscar Arias, Nobel Peace Prize laureate (1987) and former president of Costa Rica**

PROTECTING THE CHIMPANZEES

Jane Goodall's career has literally moved around the world since her first dreams of Africa. Although her early years at Gombe were marked by solitude, as she grew in prominence and the public's interest, she needed to spend more and more time away from the animals and the places she loved the most.

Goodall's efforts to spread her message of conservation now focus largely on young people. The goal of Roots and Shoots, a program she started in 1991, is to teach children both compassion for living things and responsibility for the environment and human communities.

Goodall now travels some 300 days out of every year, both to satisfy the public's demand to see her and to meet the needs of the conservation causes that she so passionately supports. Her work is not at all clear-cut, and the path sometimes leads her where she'd rather not go, but she's learned to take the bad with the good and work toward the best: "I am often accused of jumping into bed with the enemy," she has said—"we work with the timber industry, because of the trade in bush meat, and some of the oil companies. You can't force change on people. Lasting change is a series of compromises. And compromise is all right, as long your values don't change." And although her travel schedule is exhausting, Goodall says the trips leave her feeling mentally and spiritually enriched as she travels to new parts of the world, encounters new cultures, and meets new people. She would have been just as happy to stay at Gombe, but she knows she can accomplish more by spending time *away* from Africa and sees the need to try:

> My focus was learning about chimpanzees. Then my focus changed to protecting chimpanzees and making sure the research continued. Then the focus changed to youth. That was because traveling the world for the conservation message, I found so many young people who had no hope. They thought we'd compromised their future. They were right.

In October of 2001, Goodall became the third recipient of the Gandhi/King Award for Nonviolence—presented yearly by the World Movement for Nonviolence, a branch of the United Nations (U.N.)—following Kofi Annan, secretary-general of the U.N., and Nelson Mandela. Citing the state of the world since the attack of September 11, Ela Gandhi, Mahatma Gandhi's granddaughter, said, "There could not be a more deserving person than Dr. Goodall to receive this award."

She was appointed as a United Nations Messenger of Peace in April of 2002; she was the tenth high-profile person appointed to the position by Secretary-General Annan since 1997. The mission of Annan's Messengers is to encourage individuals to take responsibility for making the world a better place; they serve as advisors and advocates in such areas as disarmament, the elimination of poverty, human rights, HIV/AIDS activism, and the care of the environment. Goodall's reaction to the appointment reflects her commitment to achieving a kind of global harmony: "I am very honored to be given this responsibility at a time when the world desperately needs messages of peace and hope. In particular, I intend to carry the message that to achieve global peace, we must not only stop fighting each other but also stop destroying the natural world."

The fall of 2002 found Goodall serving on an advisory

In April of 2002, U.N. Secretary-General Kofi Annan appointed Goodall as a Messenger of Peace, charged with encouraging people to conserve nature. She is the tenth person ever to receive this honor. This photograph was taken during a ceremony held in her honor on April 16, 2002 at the U.N. headquarters in New York City.

panel to the World Summit on Sustainable Development, at Secretary-General Annan's invitation. The summit, which was held in Johannesburg, South Africa in August and September, met with the aim of motivating the world's nations to commit to finding environmentally friendly ways to develop the world's communities and to eliminate poverty. The idea was quite in line with Goodall's goals, but she was ambivalent about the expense of supporting the summit's almost 70,000 delegates: "It's horrifying to think of the waste the summit will cause. All these delegates having huge and fancy meals while so many people all around are starving. It just doesn't make sense. But I have to be here. Kofi Annan put me on his panel advising on sustainable development. So I can't avoid being here." (In fact, an organization was formed, called Greening the WSSD, to prevent damage to the city of Johannesburg.) The summit closed on September 4, 2002 with far-reaching commitments to social and environmental causes.

Much of Goodall's current work for awareness remains focused on protecting chimpanzees. According to *The Chimpanzees I Love*, African great apes are disappearing quickly: one hundred years ago there were about 2 million chimpanzees in Africa, and there probably are no more than 150,000 today. Chimpanzees are extinct in 4 of the 25 countries in which once they roamed free. And while there are more chimpanzees in the great Congo basin than anywhere else, Goodall writes, that is also where their disappearance is the most rapid. Goodall feels acutely the urgency of working through these factors, and she has made the protection of the chimps her life's work, passing her inspiration along to others each year.

THE JANE GOODALL INSTITUTE

Goodall has witnessed many of the changes that have come to the animals and land of Gombe herself in the four decades since she first stepped foot on the shores of Lake Tanganyika. When she first came to Gombe, forests rolled all along the shores of the lake and as far as one could see. Today, the 30-square-acre area within the national park remains basically untouched, but the land outside the park is scarred. All of the trees in the forests outside the park have been cut down to support the growing human population. The formerly scenic and lush hills and mountains now look like a desert, causing soil to wash down into the lake every time it rains. Today, Goodall has written, it is not enough for a scientist simply to study animals in the wild; scientists must also to try to protect animals and their natural environment.

At first, the Institute was created just to keep the research at Gombe moving forward after the kidnappings. But in addition to trying to save the 100 or so chimpanzees within the national park, Goodall and those who supported her realized they must also consider the people *outside* the park—and the damage that was being done to the land every day. To serve both purposes, the Institute has created a program whose purpose is to improve the lives of the people outside the park *while* preserving or restoring the environment. The program involves the creation of tree nurseries in 33 villages around the park, the cultivation of native plants along the base slopes, and the drilling of wells for clean water. In addition, women have new opportunities for education, and young children learn the importance of conservation. Through it all, the program aims to teach the people around Gombe to value the forests that surround them.

Expansion seems imminent for Roots and Shoots, too: Dr. Goodall made an enormously successful trip to Costa Rica in April of 2002, during which she and Dr. Oscar Arias, the former president of Costa Rica, participated in a video-conference with students in Costa Rican schools and in the Roots and Shoots program. Goodall and Arias fielded questions during this session on issues of intercultural conflict, terrorism, and the environment. Roots and Shoots may soon open a program for these and other Costa Rican students.

In addition to these programs, the Institute has created sanctuaries for infant chimps whose mothers have been shot for food. As Goodall writes in *The Chimpanzees I Love*, the young chimps usually do not have much meat on them and often are sold as pets or used to attract customers to hotels or bars. Since this is illegal in most countries, the Institute can usually persuade the local government to move the infant chimps away from such establishments and into the sanctuaries. Once there, the chimps are nursed back to health and cared for; but they can never go back to the wild. Other chimps may attack them, or the nursed infants may wander into villages and hurt, or be hurt by, the inhabitants, since by this point the chimps usually have lost their fear of humans. So far, the Institute has created chimp sanctuaries in Congo-Brazzaville, Uganda, and Kenya. The people at the Institute are also building a sanctuary in South Africa.

Today, the Jane Goodall Institute maintains field offices in ten countries on four continents. It works not only to preserve the way of life of chimps in the wild and to improve the conditions under which they live in captivity, but also to foster a sense of human responsibility for the environment. The Institute continues Goodall's research at Gombe—a particular center is devoted to the analysis of her 40 years of data—and has undertaken a major reforestation project in Tanzania. It also fights, as part of a larger organization, to end the trade in "bushmeat" that threatens the lives of so many chimps.

There were many, Goodall writes, who did not encourage her to get involved with orphan chimps:

> It would be costly, and we would have to care for them throughout their long lives (as long as sixty years), for they can almost never be returned to the wild. It would be better, I was told, to use the previous dollars to try to save the wild chimpanzees and their habitat. Others felt I should help the African people rather than "mere" animals. But for me there was no dilemma. I could not turn my back on the outstretched hands, the pleading eyes, the pathetic malnourished bodies of the orphans.
>
> (*Reason*, 210)

But since its creation, the sanctuary program has become a central part of the Institute's conservation education program. It is especially popular with children.

THE THREATENED CHIMPANZEE

Dr. Goodall's *The Chimpanzees I Love* cites several reasons for the chimps' disappearance:

- Their forest homes are being destroyed all over Africa. As the population of humans grows and humans take more land and wood for their farms and homes.

- They can be caught in traps meant for bushpigs or antelopes. While the chimpanzees can sometimes break the wire of the trap, they can't free themselves from the noose. Some of these chimps die, and others lose limbs after months of pain.

- Dealers smuggle them out of Africa for sale. Sometimes, chimp mothers are shot so their infants can be taken for entertainment or medical research. Many chimps die in the forest—including those males who try to protect the young one—for just one infant chimp to make it to sale alive. The chimp dealers pay the hunters just a few dollars for each chimp and then sell the chimps for $2,000 each or more.

- They are killed by commercial hunters. Commercial hunting for food is the greatest threat to the chimpanzees in the great Congo basin. Local tribes have coexisted with animals in the forests for hundreds of years, but today logging companies have moved deep into the last remaining forests. Hunters from these companies ride trucks to the end of the road and shoot everything they can—chimps, gorillas, bonobos, elephants, antelopes, and even birds. Many residents of larger towns prefer the taste of wild animals and are willing to pay high prices.

Although her work now focuses on meeting with the public and spreading the message of conservation, Goodall does sometimes get to share a moment with her beloved chimps. "We shall not let the chimpanzees become extinct in Africa," she vows, "and we shall not let them go on being cruelly treated in captivity."

Goodall has worked extensively with young people to use their enthusiasm and concern to make a difference. In *The Chimpanzees I Love*, Goodall writes:

> The most important message I have for you is that you, as an individual, can make a difference every day of your life. And you can choose what sort of difference you want to make. People ask me why I have so much hope for the future when things often seem grim. I'll tell you. ... I have hope for the future because of the energy and commitment and persistence of young people around the globe. I get so excited when I hear what all the Roots and Shoots groups are doing to make the world a better

place. . . . We shall not let the chimpanzees become extinct in Africa, and we shall not let them go on being cruelly treated in captivity.

(*The Chimpanzees I Love*, 71, 73)

In *Reason for Hope*, Goodall says she had four reasons for maintaining hope even when facing the most difficult challenges: the human brain, the resilience of nature, the energy and enthusiasm that is found or can be stirred in young people around the world, and the strength of the human spirit. And at the end of *The Chimpanzees I Love*, Goodall writes a final message of inspiration. As a small child, she says, she never imagined how her life would be changed, and made richer, by the time she spent living with the chimpanzees of Gombe. "I hope your life, too, will be richer for knowing about them," she writes, "and I hope you will be inspired, as I was, to do all you can to make the world a better place for all living things."

Chronology

1934 Born on April 3 in London, England, to Margaret Myfanwe Joseph and Mortimer Herbert Morris-Goodall.

1951 Graduates from high school. Spends the fall and early winter living with a family in Germany.

1952 Enrolls in a secretarial school in London.

1953 Hired to work for Oxford University Registry in August.

1956 Receives a letter from her best friend from school, inviting her to visit her in Africa.

1957 Arrives in Nairobi on April 3. Meets Louis Leakey.

1958 Returns to England in December.

1960 Flies to Nairobi with her mother in May to begin studying the chimpanzees at Gombe National Park. Makes first major discoveries that year.

1961 Returns to England in December to begin doctoral studies at Cambridge University. Splits time over the next few years between Gombe and Cambridge.

1963 Article on Goodall and the chimpanzees of Gombe is published in *National Geographic*. Becomes engaged to Hugo van Lawick in December.

1964 Is married to van Lawick.

1965–66 First semi-permanent buildings are erected at Gombe.

1966 Receives Ph.D. from Cambridge University; meets Dian Fossey in December.

1967 Son Hugo Eric Louis van Lawick ("Grub") is born on March 4.

1971	Is appointed Visiting Professor of Psychiatry and Human Biology at Stanford University.
1974	Is divorced from Hugo van Lawick.
1975	Marries Derek Bryceson. Four researchers at Gombe are kidnapped in May and later released.
1977	Founds the Jane Goodall Institute for Wildlife Research, Education, and Conservation.
1980	Bryceson dies of cancer.
1986	*The Chimpanzees of Gombe* is published to great acclaim.
1987	Visits first biomedical research laboratory. Becomes an advocate for humane treatment of research animals.
1990–99	Publishes three adult-market books and one children's book. Founds Roots and Shoots.
2001	Publishes children's book *The Chimpanzees I Love*.
2002	Accepts appointment by U.N. Secretary General Kofi Annan as a United Nations Messenger of Peace on April 16.

Bibliography

Dreifus, Claudia. "Jane of the Jungle." *Modern Maturity*, Nov./Dec. 1999.

Goodall, Jane. *Africa in My Blood: An Autobiography in Letters (vol. 1)*. Ed. Dale Peterson. Boston: Houghton Mifflin, 2000.

———. *Beyond Innocence: An Autobiography in Letters (vol. 2)*. Ed. Dale Peterson. Boston: Houghton Mifflin, 2001.

———. *The Chimpanzees I Love: Saving Their World and Ours*. New York: Scholastic Press, 2001.

———. *My Life with the Chimpanzees*. New York: Simon and Schuster, 1988. Revised edition, Minstrel Books, 1996.

———. *Reason for Hope: A Spiritual Journey*. New York: Time Warner Books, 1999. Paperback edition, New York: Warner Books, 2000.

———. *In the Shadow of Man*. Boston: Houghton Mifflin, 1971. Revised paperback edition, 1988.

———. *Through a Window: 30 Years Observing the Gombe Chimpanzees*. Boston: Houghton Mifflin, 1990.

Works by Jane Goodall

My Friends the Wild Chimpanzees, 1967

Innocent Killers, 1970

In the Shadow of Man, 1971

The Chimpanzees of Gombe: Patterns of Behaviour, 1984

Through a Window: 30 Years Observing the Gombe Chimpanzees, 1987

Visions of Caliban: On Chimpanzees and People, 1993

Jane Goodall: With Love, 1994

Reason for Hope: A Spiritual Journey, 1999

Africa in My Blood: An Autobiography in Letters (vol. 1), 2000

40 Years at Gombe: A Tribute to Four Decades of Wildlife Research, Education, and Conservation, 2000

Beyond Innocence: An Autobiography in Letters (vol. 2), 2001

The Ten Trusts: What We Must Do to Care for the Animals We Love, 2002

Articles (Partial Listing)

"My Life With the Wild Chimpanzees." *National Geographic* 124(2): 272–308, 1963.

"New Discoveries among Africa's Chimpanzees." *National Geographic* 128(6):802–831, 1965.

"Life and Death at Gombe." *National Geographic* 155(5):592–621, 1979.

"Mountain Warrior." *Omni* (May 1986): 132–143.

"A Plea for the Chimps." *The New York Sunday Times Magazine* (May 17, 1987): 108–110.

For Children

Grub: The Bush Baby, 1971

My Life with the Chimpanzees, 1988

The Chimpanzee Family Book, 1989

Jane Goodall's Animal World: Chimps, 1989

Animal Family series, 1991

> *Baboon Family*
>
> *Chimpanzee Family*
>
> *Elephant Family*
>
> *Giraffe Family*

Hyena Family
Lion Family
Wildebeest Family
Zebra Family
Dr. White, 1999
The Eagle and the Wren, 2000
The Chimpanzees I Love: Saving Their World and Ours, 2001

Films

Miss Goodall and the Wild Chimpanzees, 1963
Among the Wild Chimpanzees, 1984
Chimpanzee Alert, 1990
Chimps, So Like Us, 1990
The Life and Legend of Jane Goodall, 1990
The Gombe Chimpanzees, 1990 (Bavaria)
Fifi's Boys, 1995 (BBC)
Chimpanzee Diary, 1997 (BBC)
Jane Goodall's Wild Chimpanzees, 2002 (IMAX)

de Waal, Franz, and Frans Lanting. *Bonobo: The Forgotten Ape.* Berkeley: University of California Press, 1998.

Fossey, Dian. *Gorillas in the Mist.* New York: Mariner, 2000.

Fromer, Julie. *Jane Goodall: Living the Chimps.* Frederick, Maryland: Twenty-First Century Books, 1992.

Iwago, Mitsuaki. *Serengeti: Natural Order on the African Plain.* San Francisco: Chronicle, 1996.

Leakey, Richard. *Origins Reconsidered: In Search of What Makes Us Human.* Homer, Alaska: Anchor, 1993.

Lucas, Eileen. *Jane Goodall, Friend of the Chimps.* Brookfield, Connecticut: Millbrook Press, 1992.

Montgomery, Sy. *Walking with the Great Apes: Jane Goodall, Dian Fossey, Birute Galdikas.* New York: Houghton Mifflin, 1991.

Morell, Virginia. *Ancestral Passions: The Leakey Family and the Quest for Humankind's Beginnings.* New York: Touchstone, 1996.

Mowat, Farley. *Woman in the Mists: The Story of Dian Fossey and the Mountain Gorillas of Africa.* New York: Warner, 1988.

Newkirk, Ingrid. *You Can Save the Animals: 251 Ways to Stop Thoughtless Cruelty.* Roseville, California: Prima, 1999.

Websites

The Jane Goodall Institute
www.janegoodall.org

ChimpanZoo
chimpanzoo.arizona.edu

Lessons for Hope
www.lessonsforhope.org

The Jane Goodall Center for Excellence in Environmental Studies
www.wcsu.ctstateu.edu/cyberchimp/homepage.html

National Geographic: Famous Faces: Jane Goodall
www.nationalgeographic.com/faces/goodall/

Jane Goodall Exhibit: Discovering Chimpanzees: The Remarkable
World of Jane Goodall
www.discoveringchimpanzees.com

Discovering Chimpanzees
www.sciencenorth.ca/chimp/

Discover Chimpanzees!
www.discoverchimpanzees.org

Discovering Chimps
biosci.cbs.umn.edu/chimp/

The Jane Goodall Institute: Roots & Shoots
P.O. Box 14890
Silver Springs, MD 20911

The Association for Women in Science
1200 New York Ave., Suite 650 NW
Washington, DC USA 20005
202.326.8940
www.awis.org

Index

Index

Index

Index

Picture Credits

Contributors

LISA KOZLESKI is a newspaper reporter at *The Morning Call* in Allentown, Pennsylvania, and has worked for newspapers in Colorado, Washington, Philadelphia, and England. She moved in 1995 to the Philadelphia area, where she lives with her husband, John Harding, and their dog, Kaia. This is her fourth book for young readers.

JILL SIDEMAN, PH.D. serves as vice president of CH2M HILL, an international environmental-consulting firm based in San Francisco. She was among the few women to study physical chemistry and quantum mechanics in the late 1960s and conducted over seven years of post-doctoral research in high-energy physics and molecular biology. In 1974, she co-founded a woman-owned environmental-consulting firm that became a major force in environmental-impact analysis, wetlands and coastal zone management, and energy conservation. She went on to become Director of Environmental Planning and Senior Client Service Manager at CH2M HILL. An active advocate of women in the sciences, she was elected in 2001 as president of the Association for Women in Science, a national organization "dedicated to achieving equity and full participation for women in science, mathematics, engineering and technology."